The Artwork of Presedo²

Illustrations by Daniel Lavagna Presedo

Twitter | Instagram | YouTube | Etsy
@dramenon

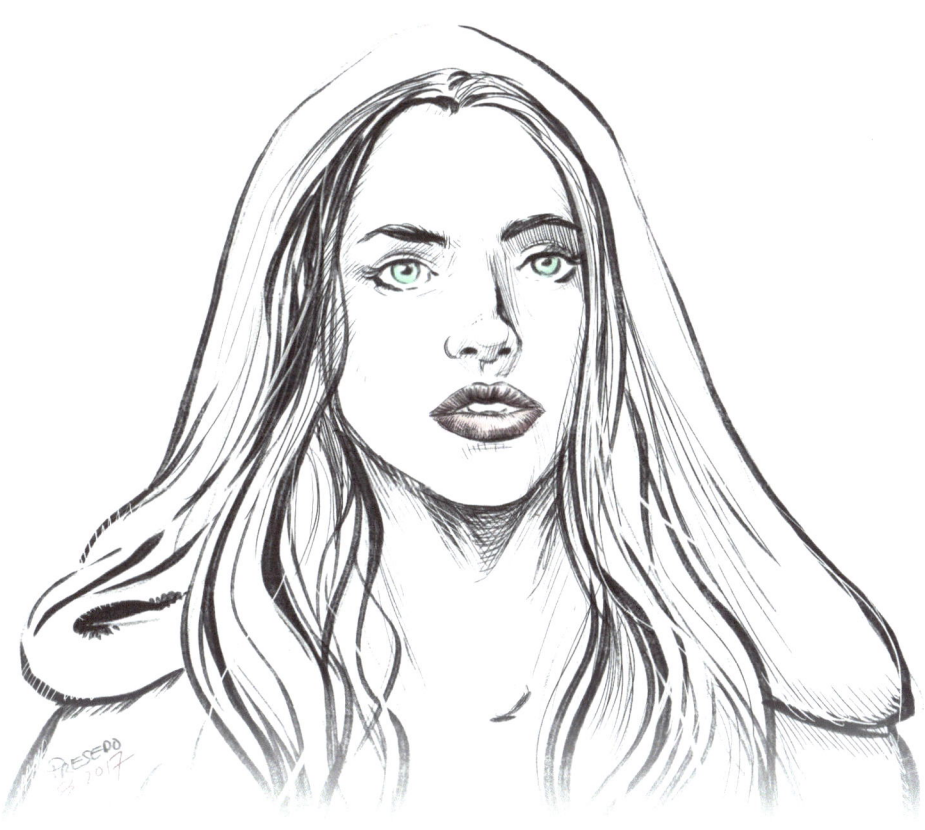

The Art of Presedo 2 - Volume One is © 2017 to Dramenon Studios LLC. This is a work of fiction. The art and characters, incidents, and dialogues are products of the author's imagination and are not to be construed as real. Any resemblance to actual events or persons, living or dead, is entirely coincidental. None of the contents may be reprinted, except for purposes of review, without the written permission of Dramenon Studios LLC. www.dramenon.com

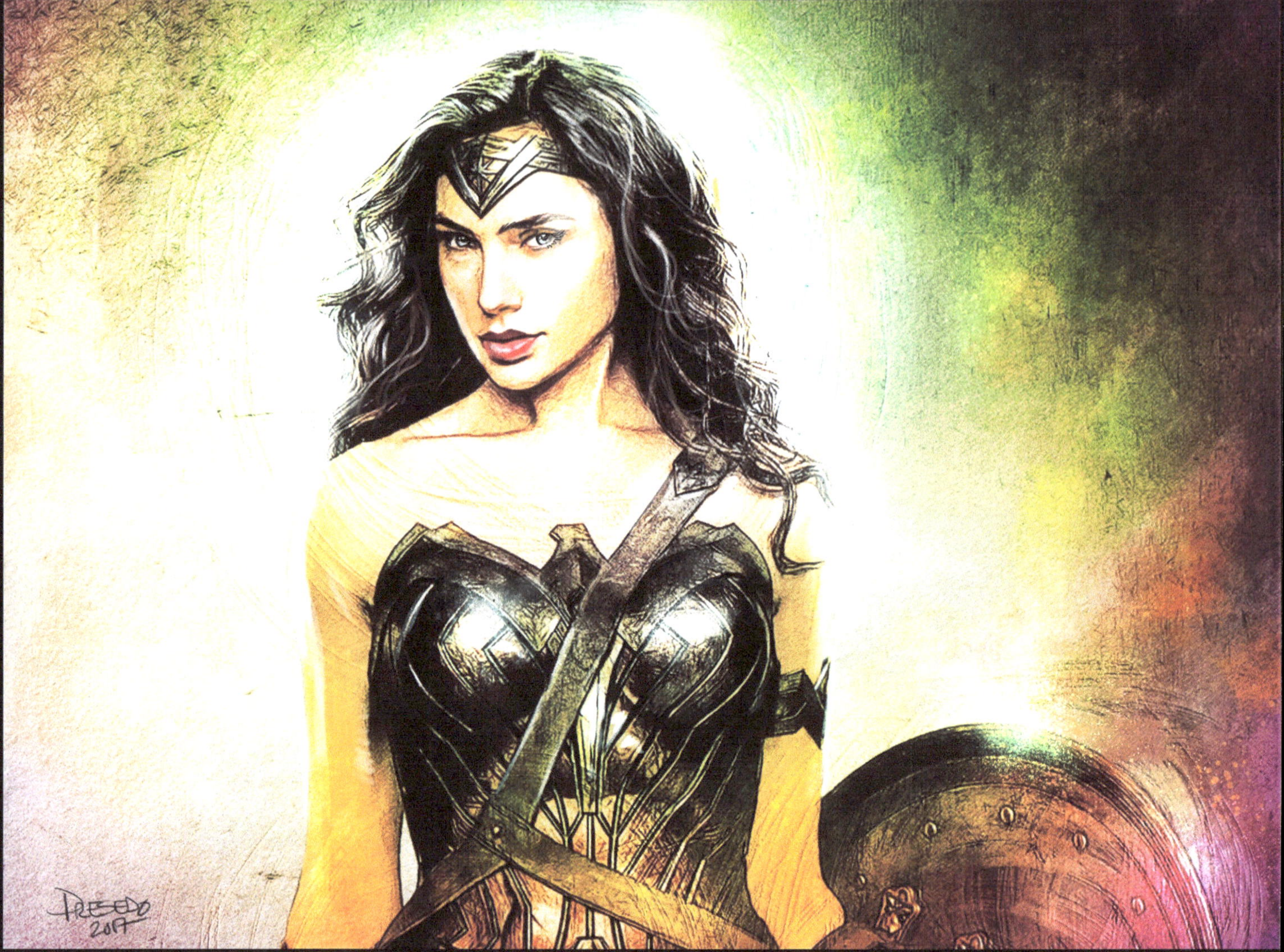

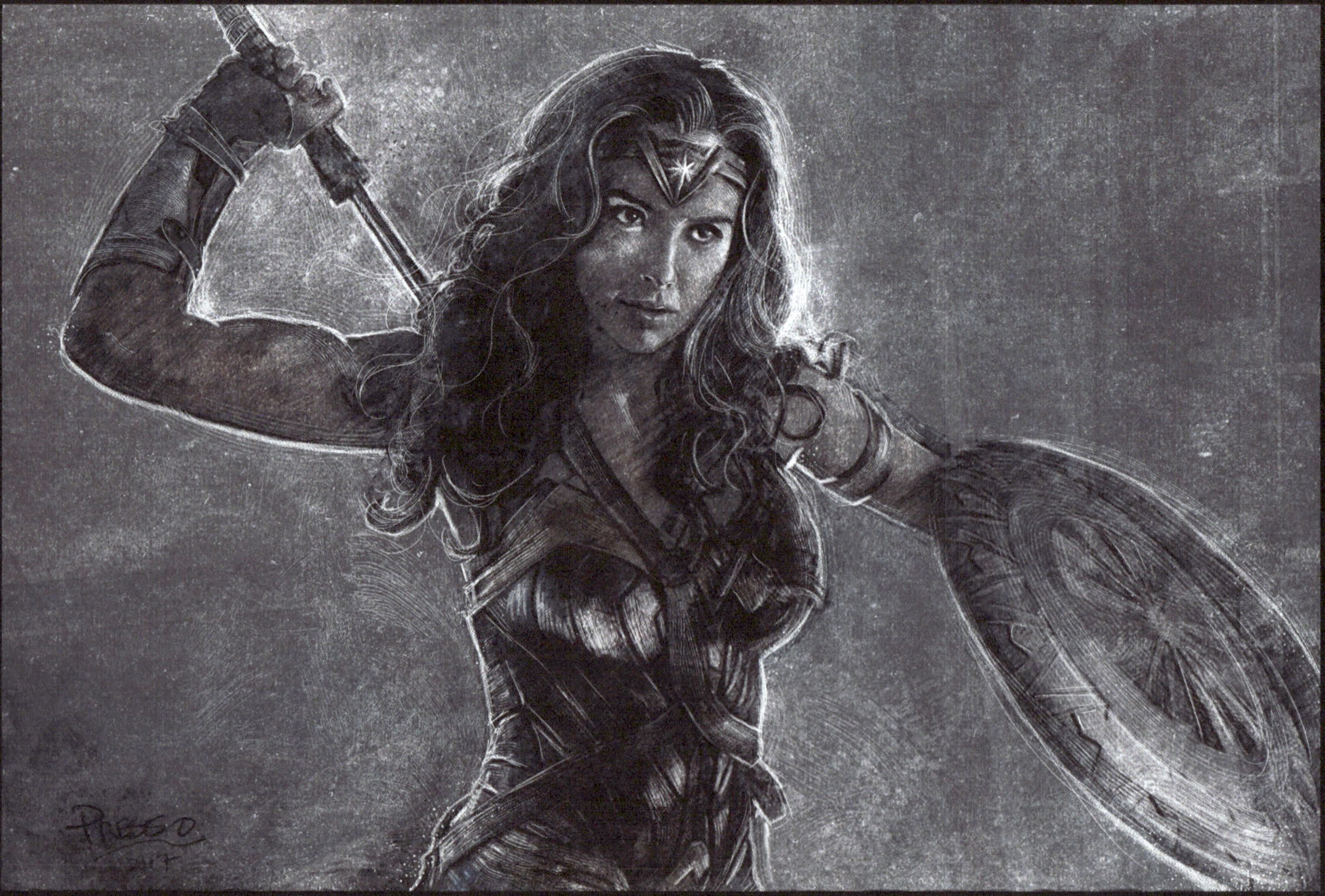

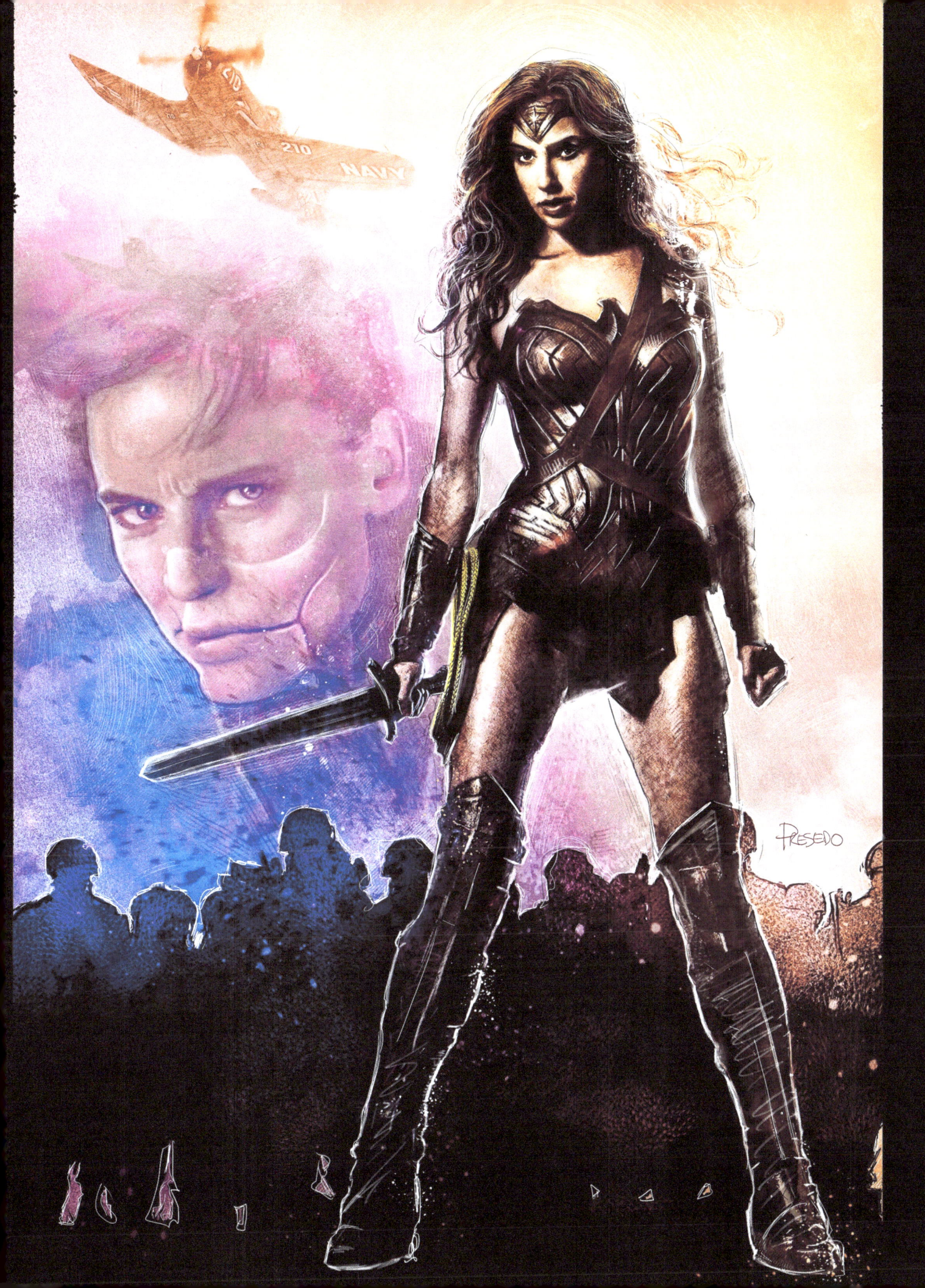

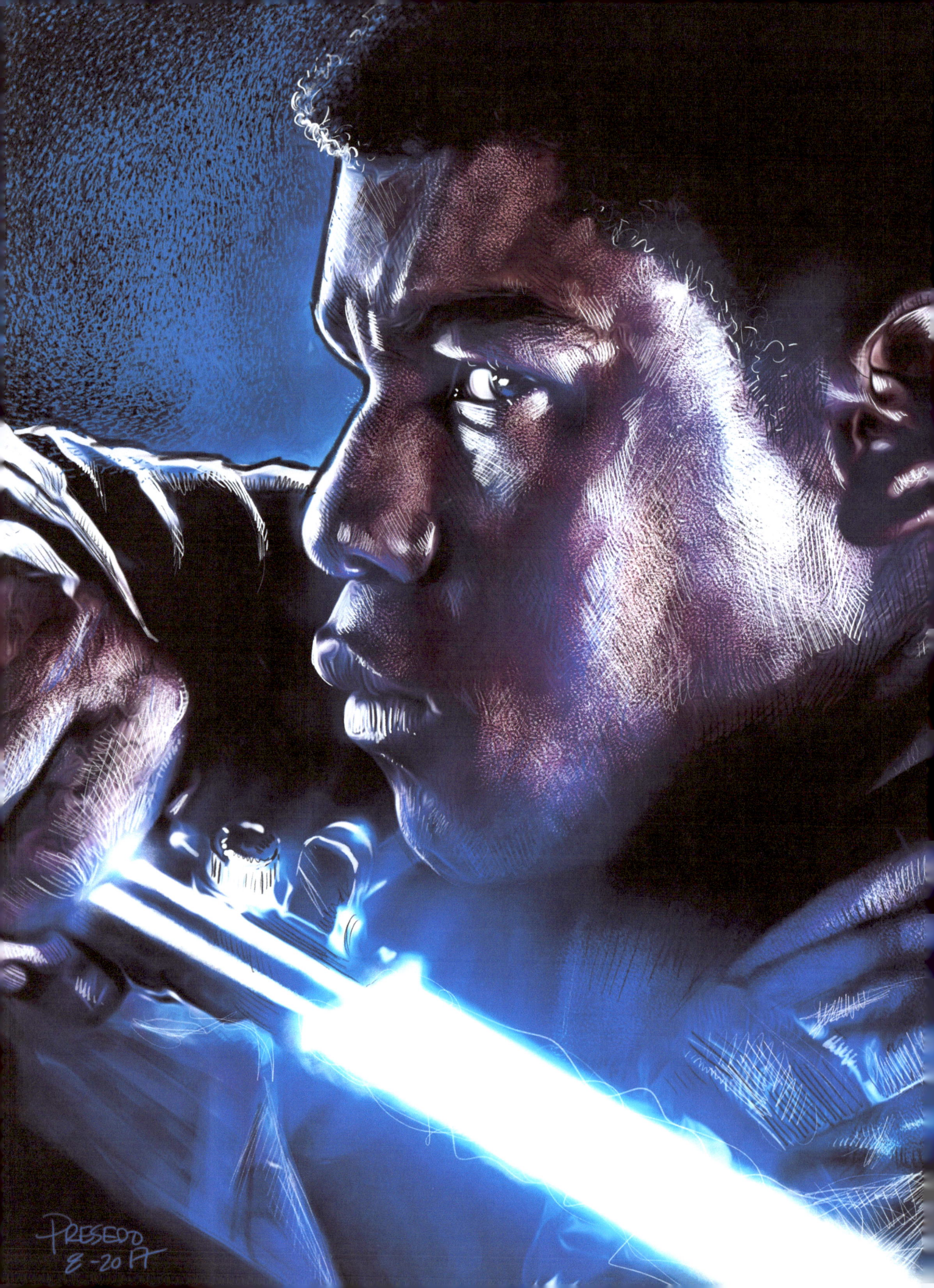

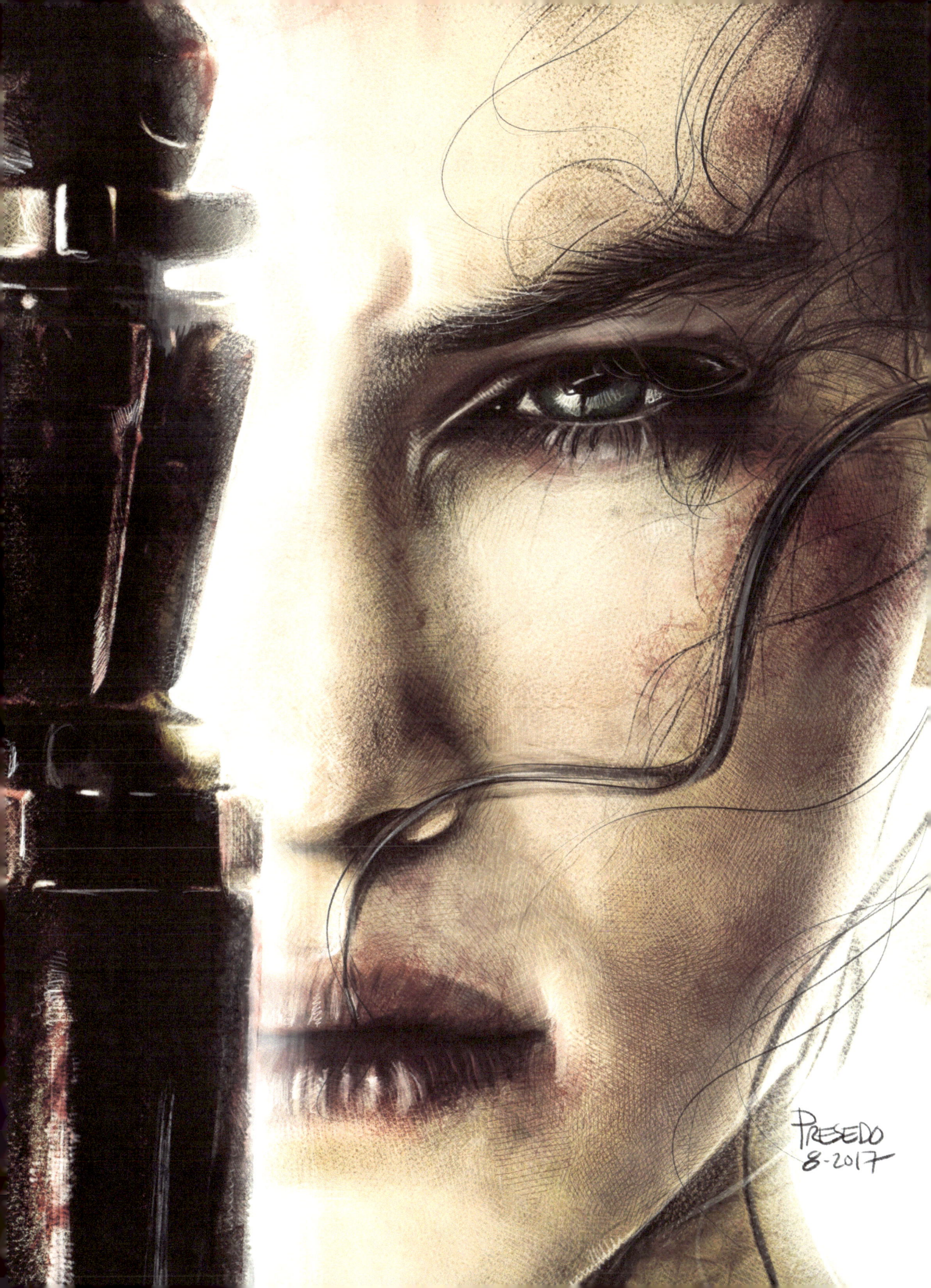

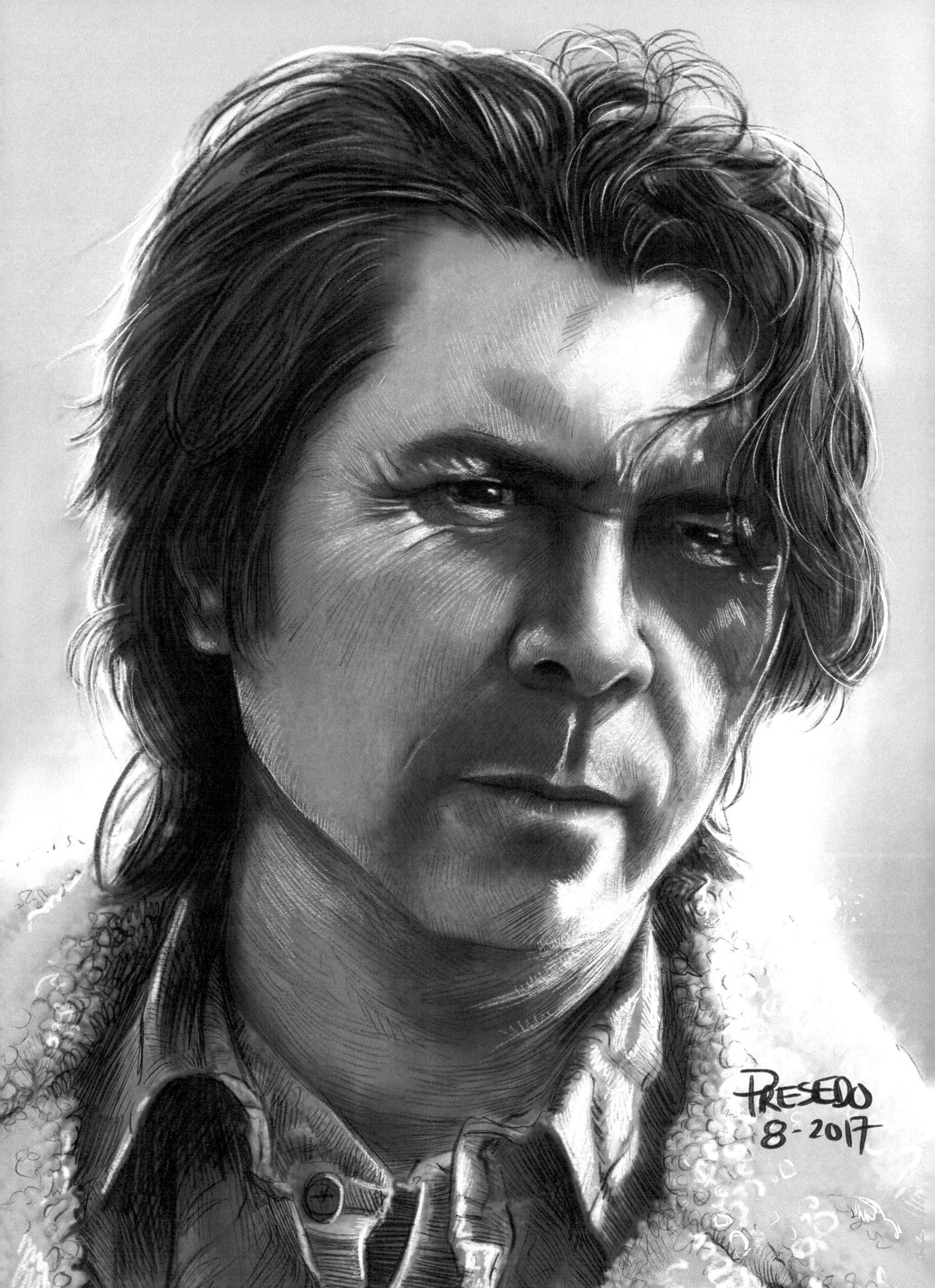

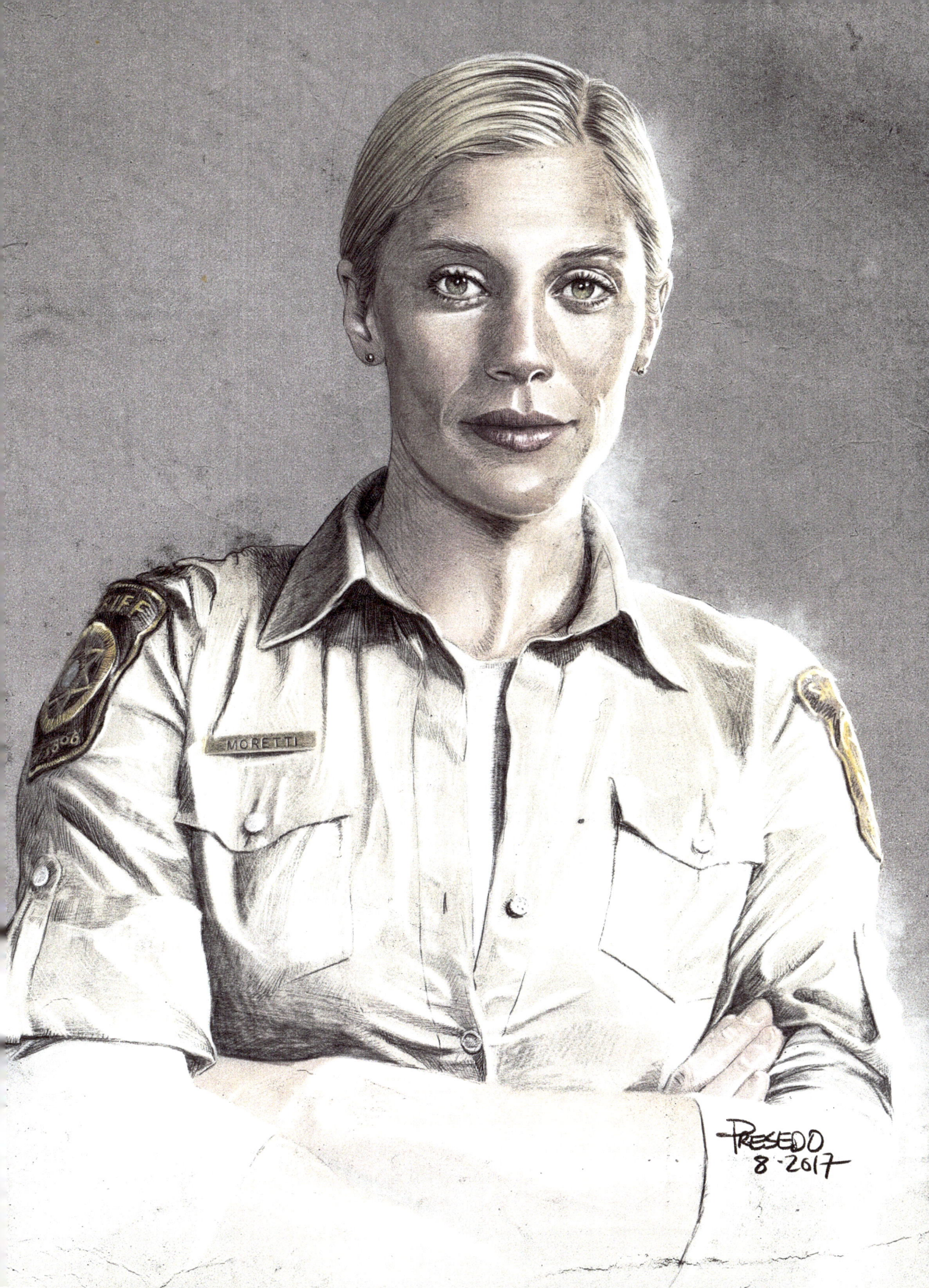

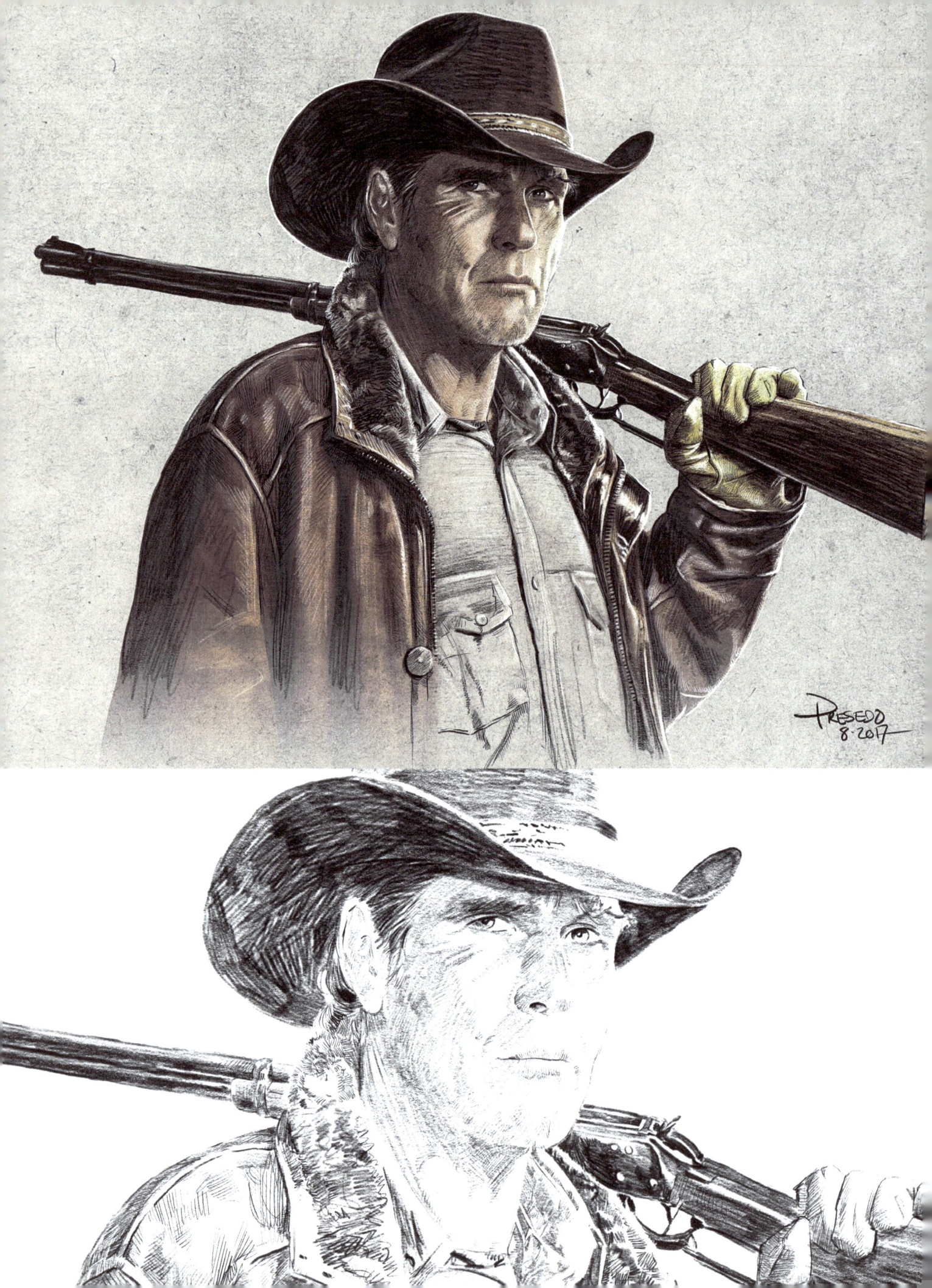

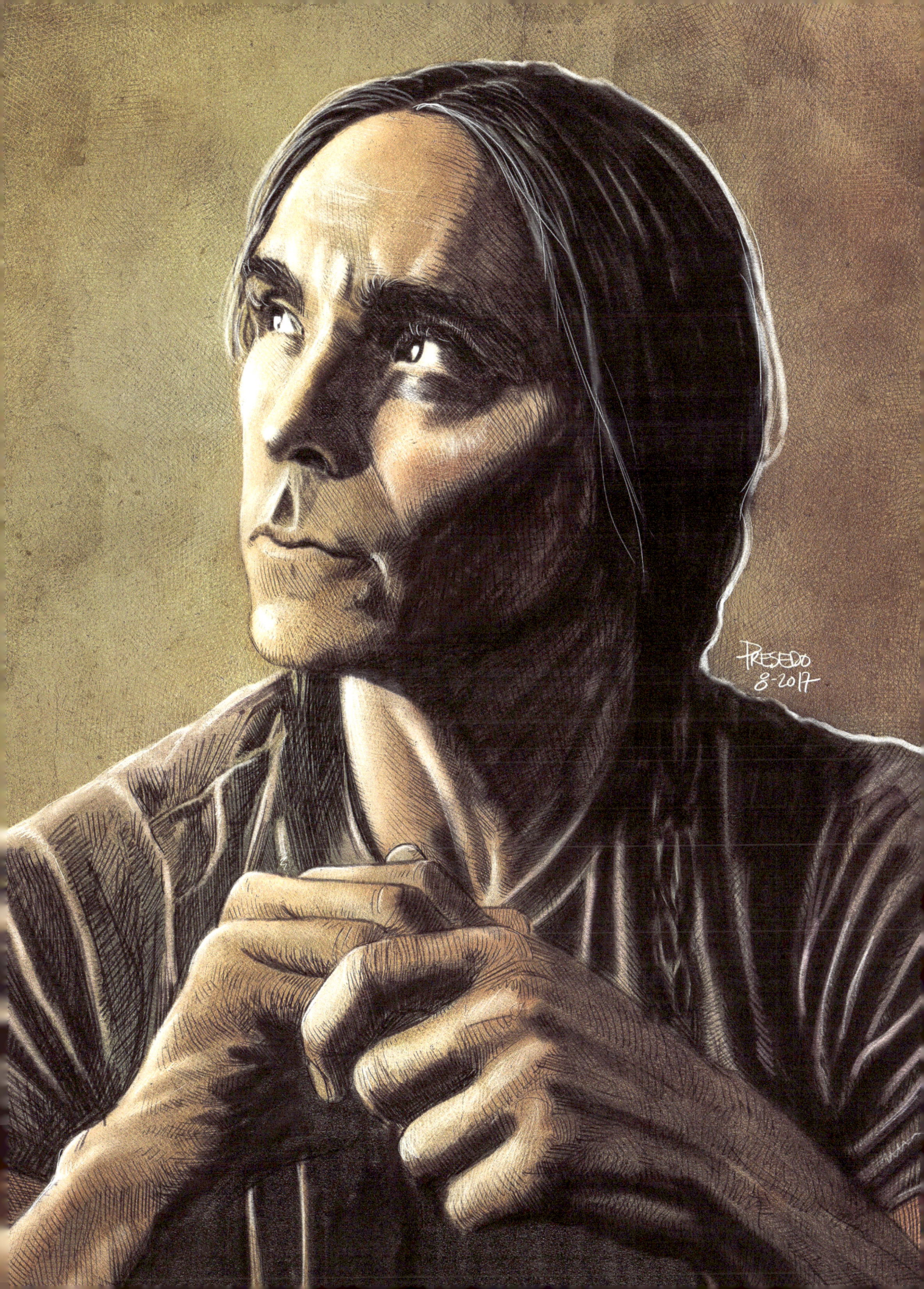

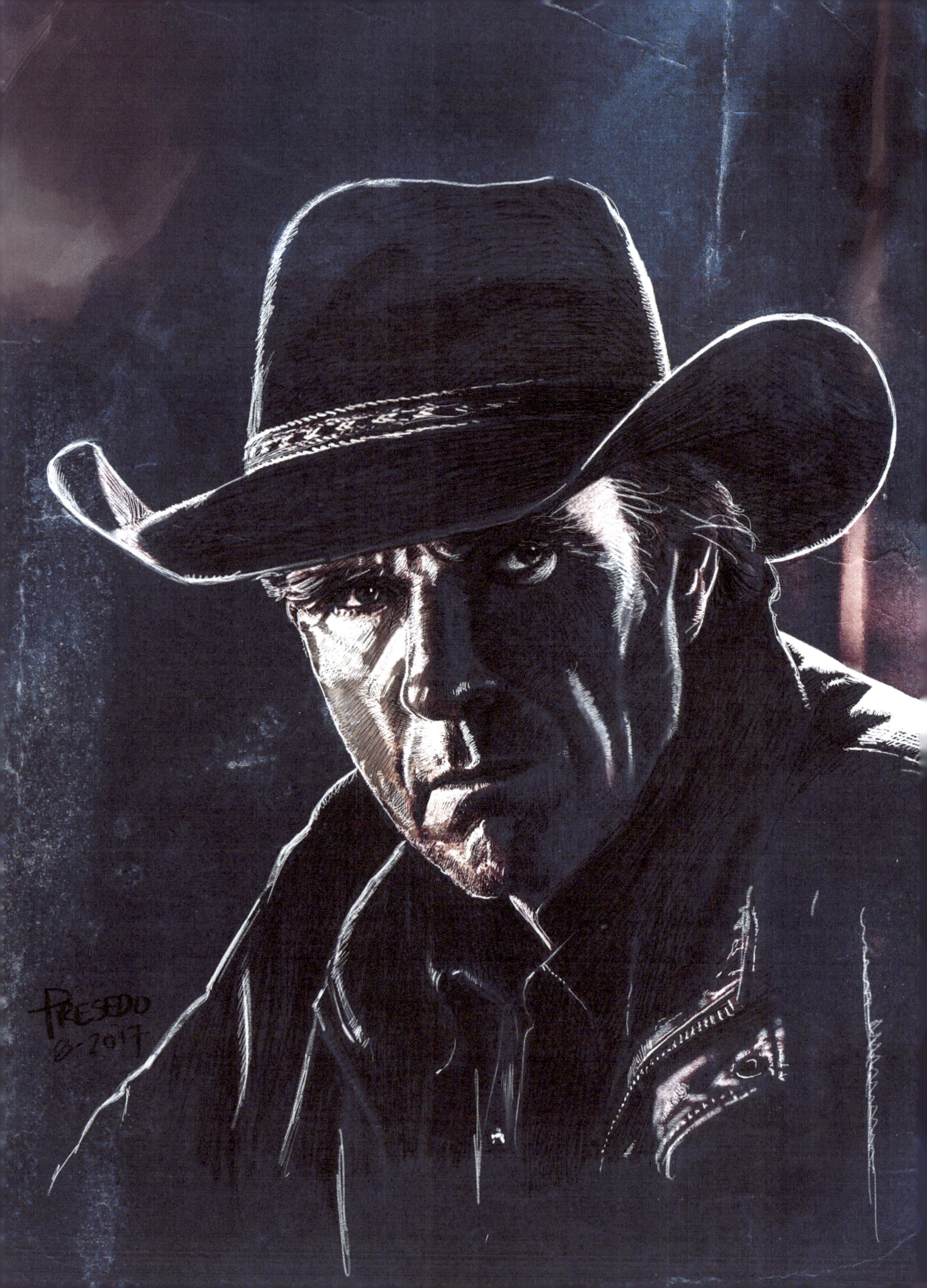

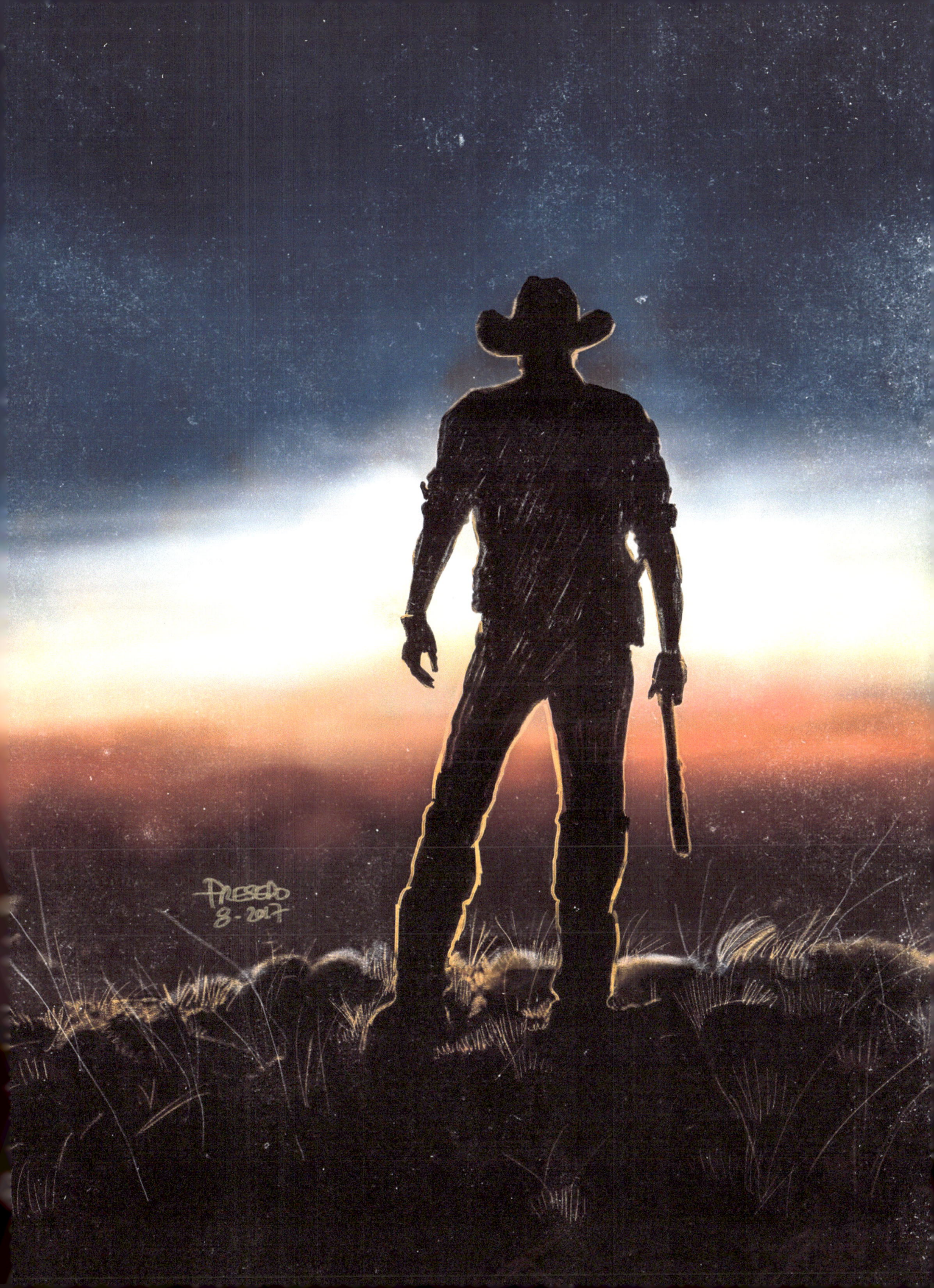

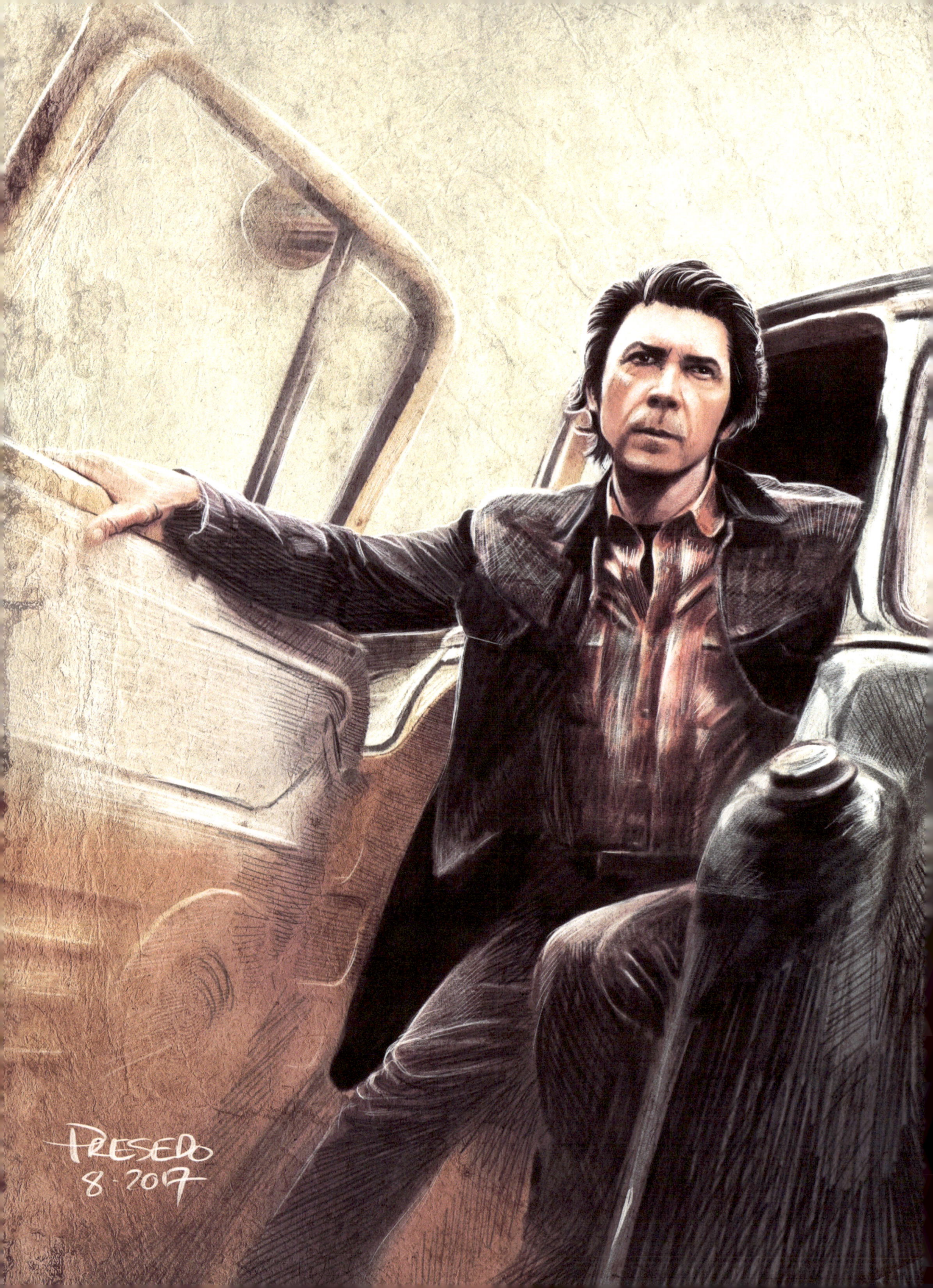

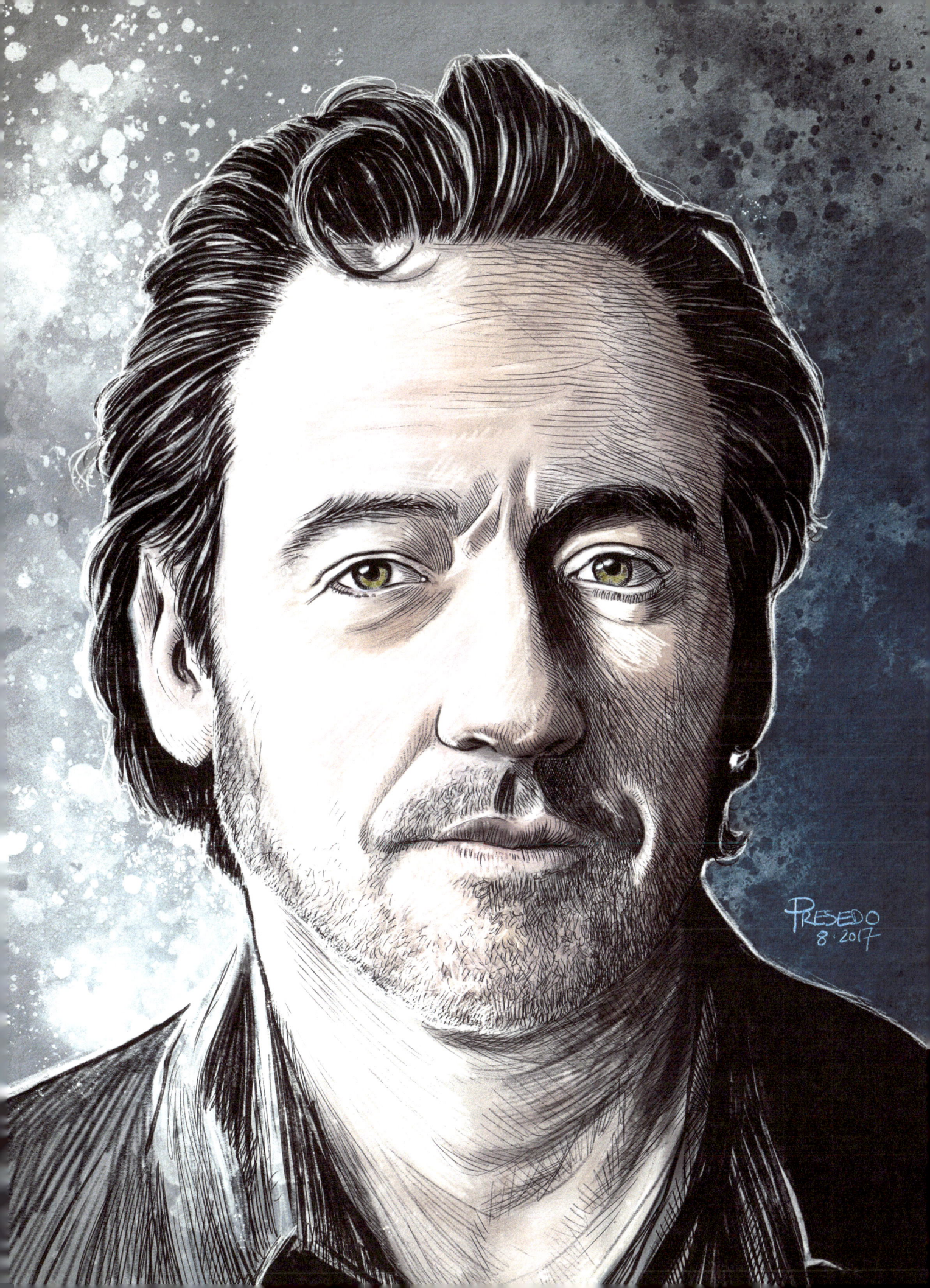

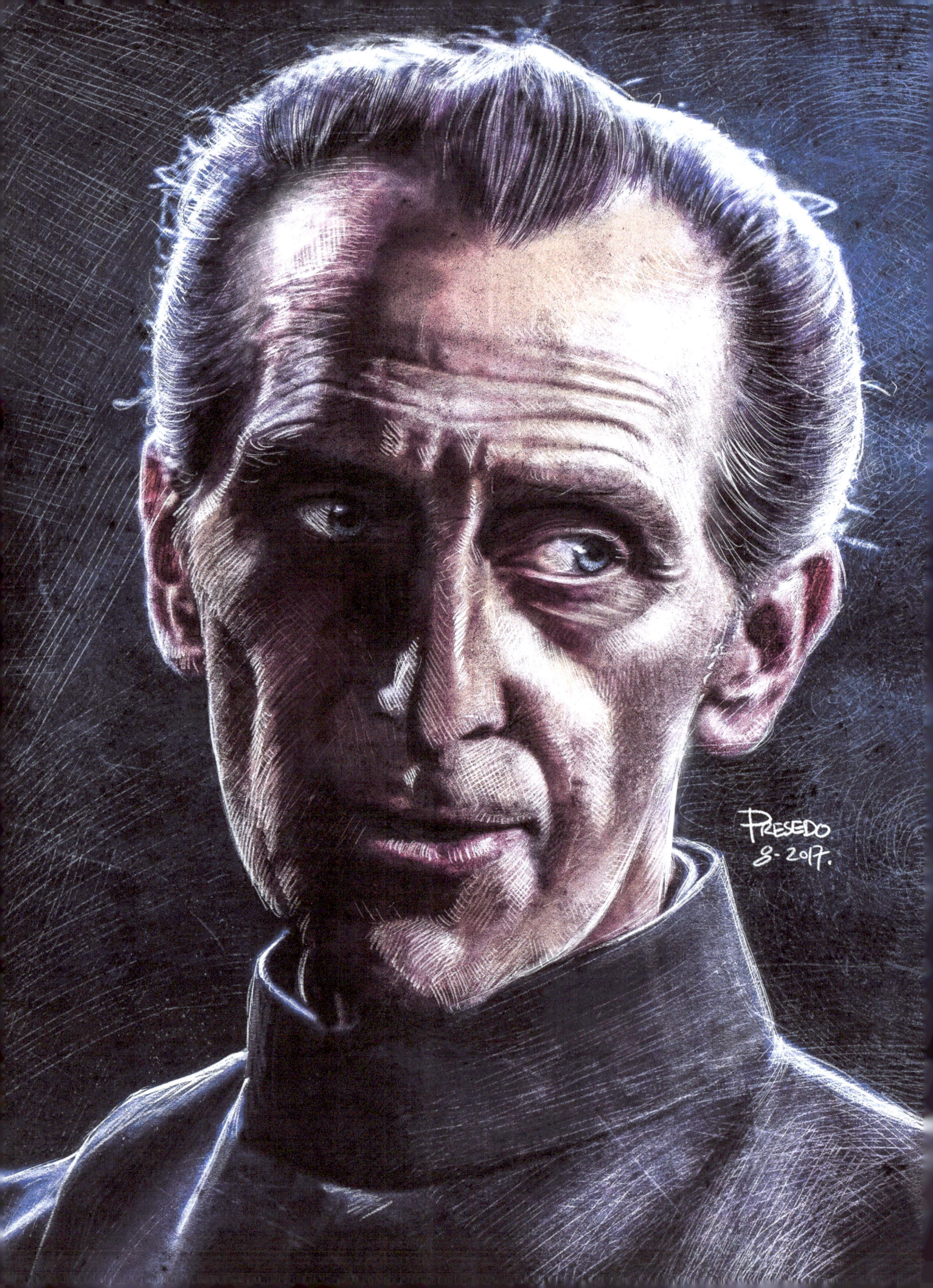

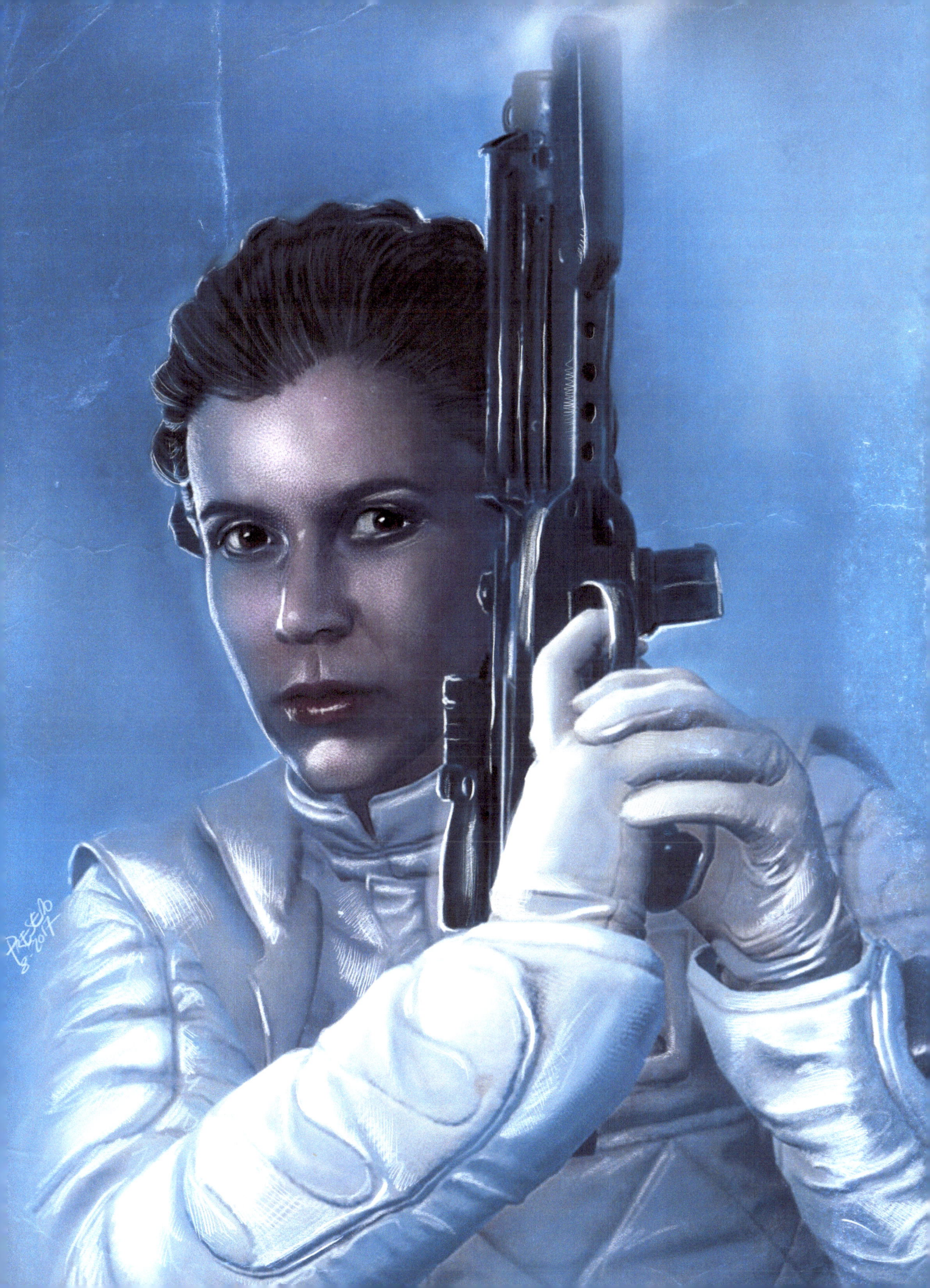

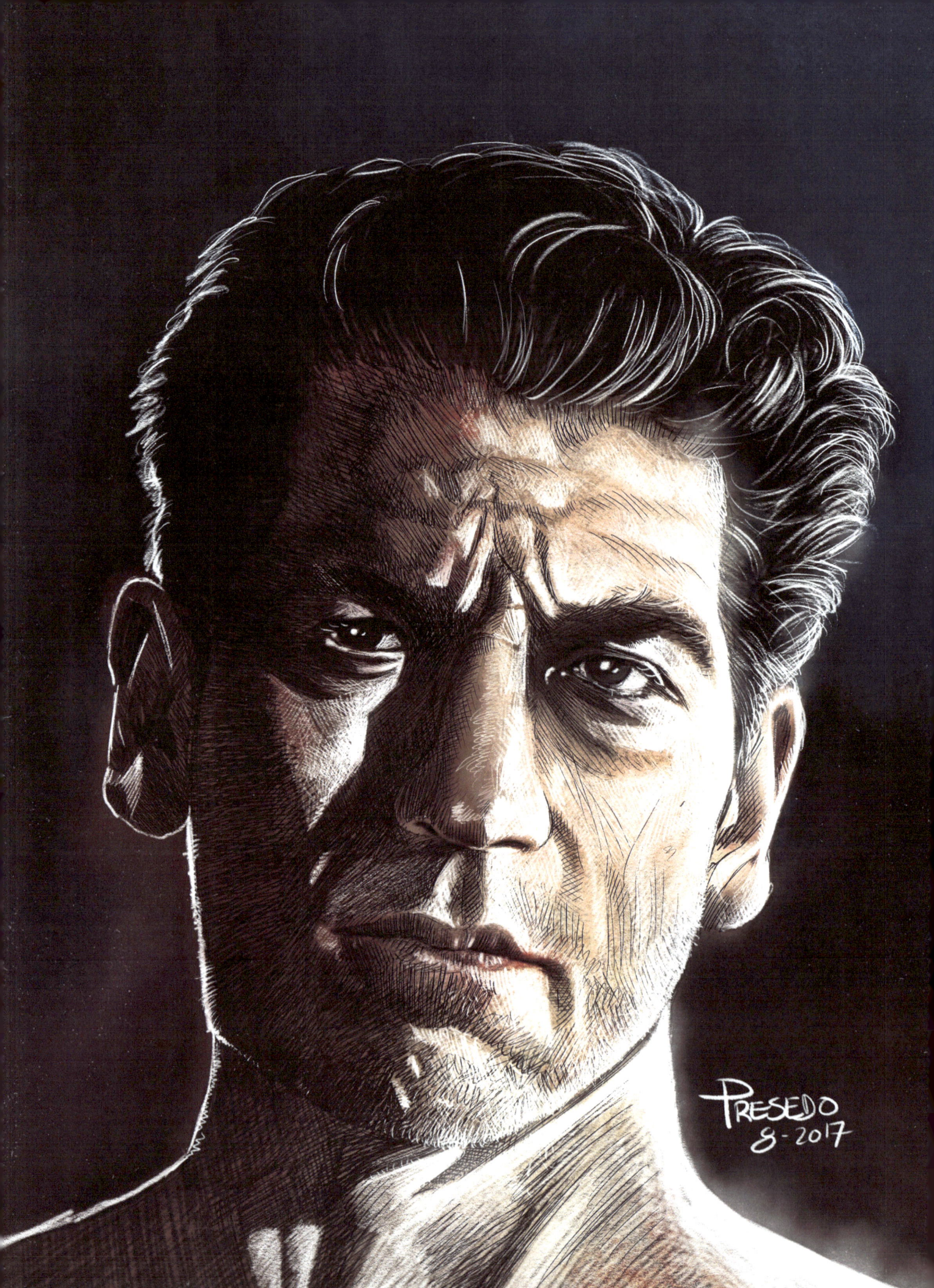

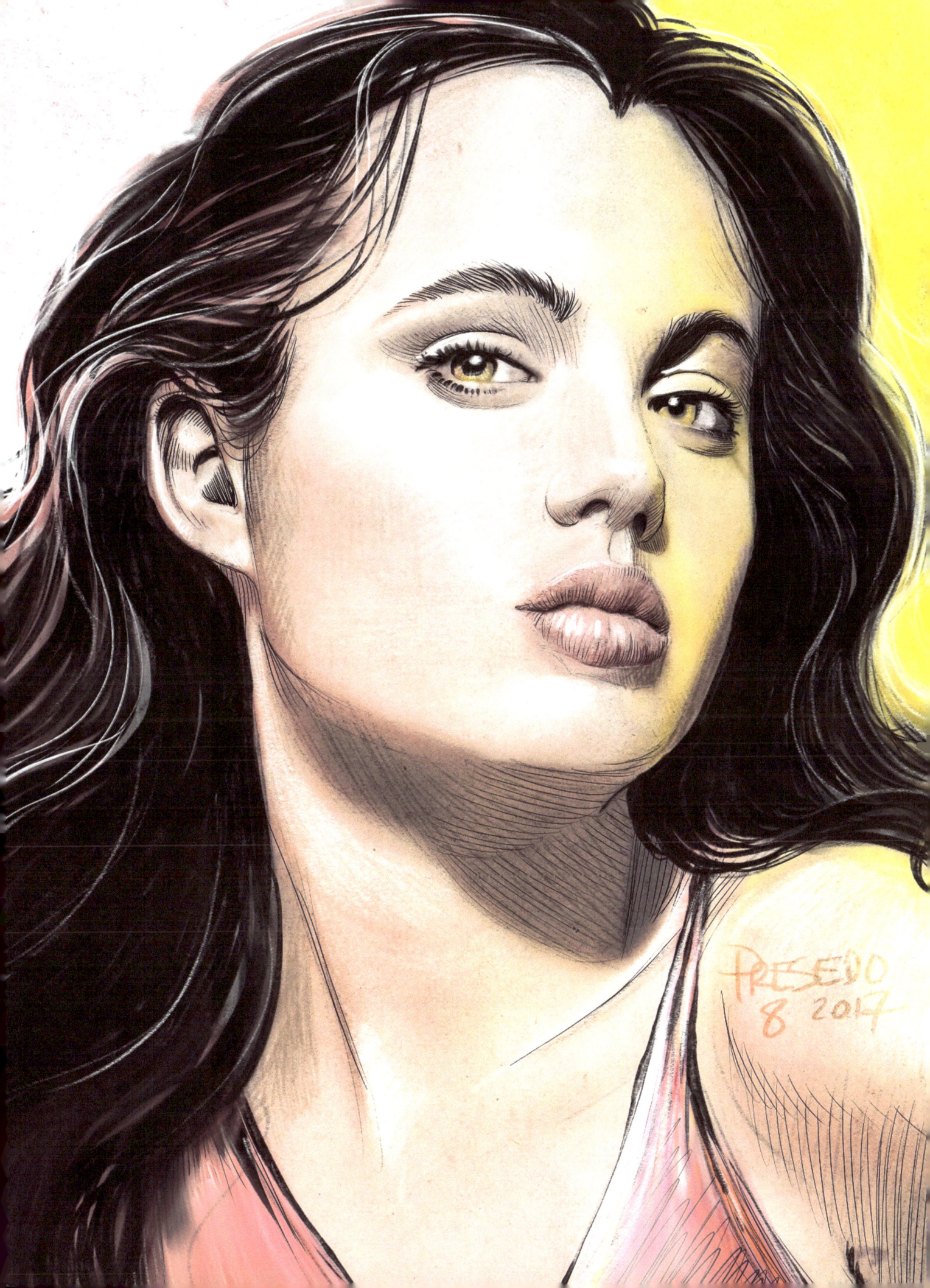

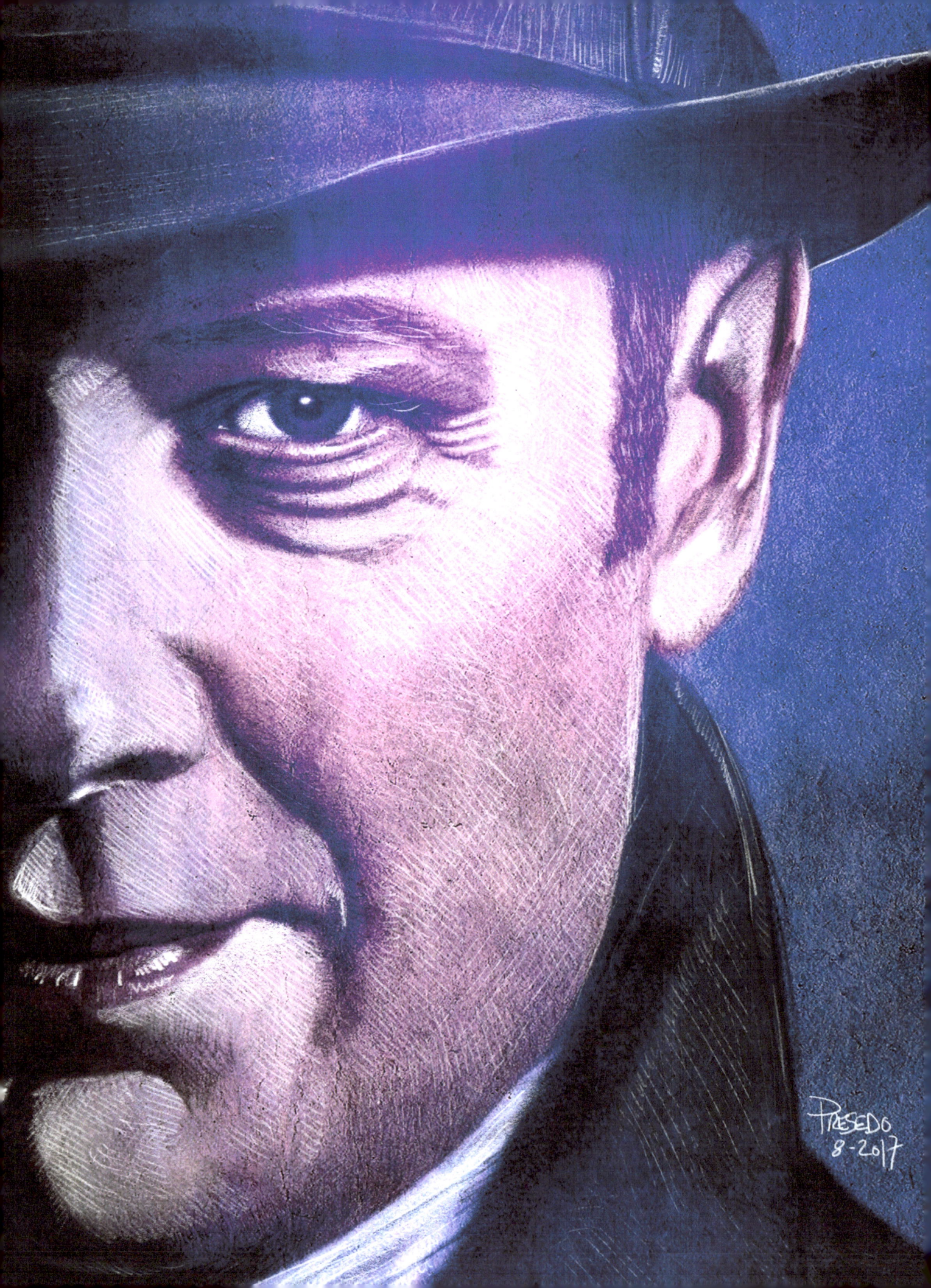

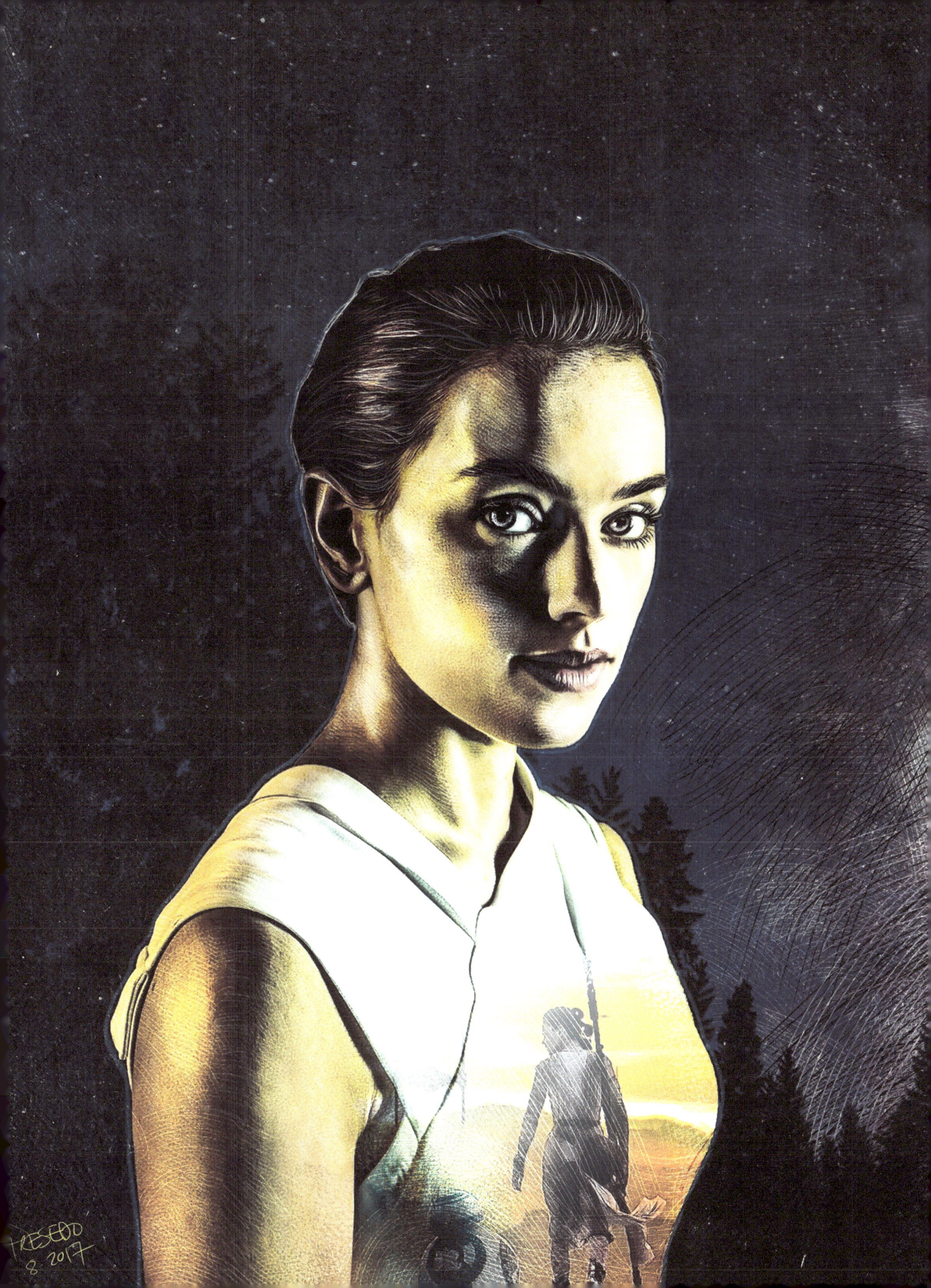

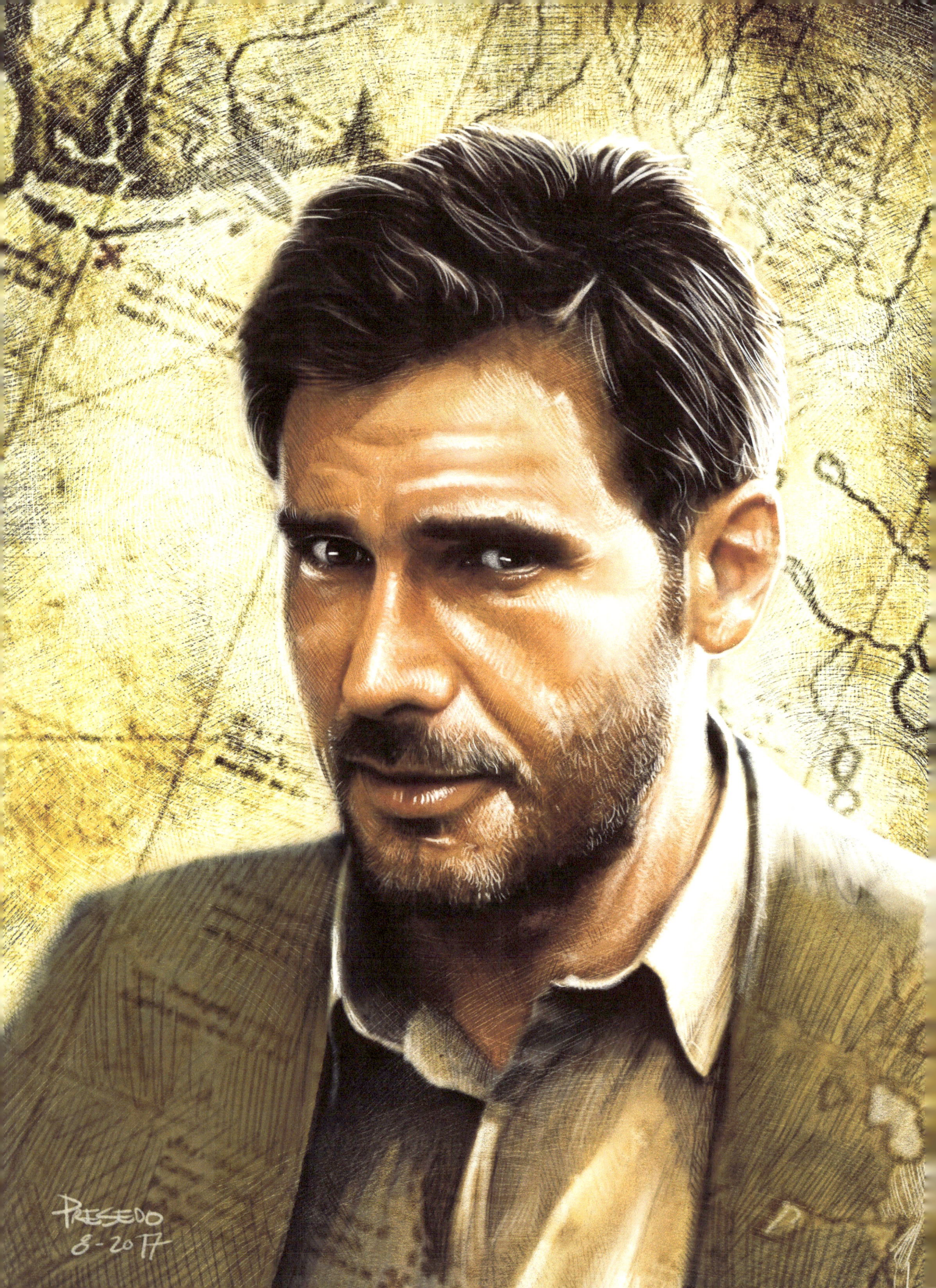

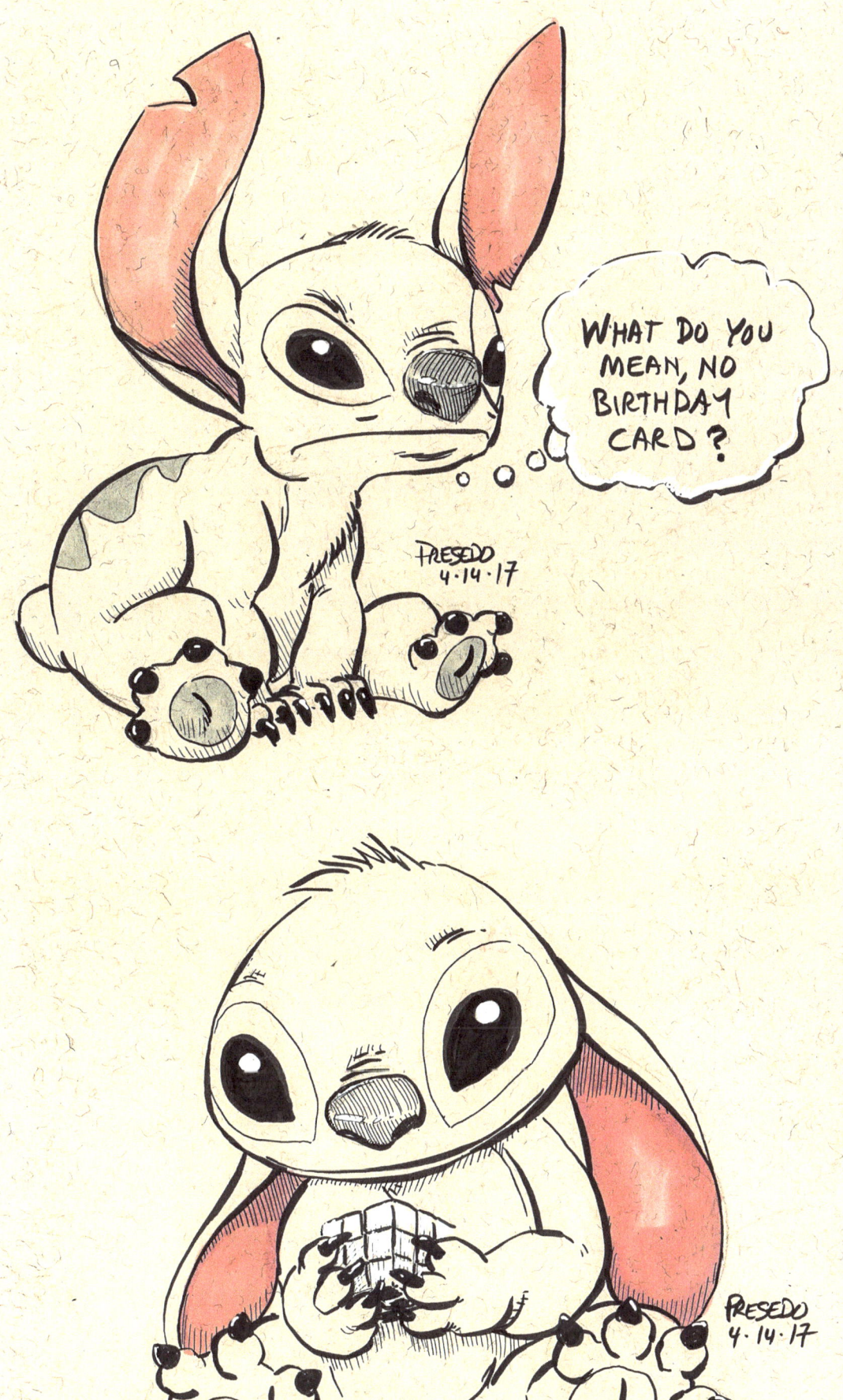

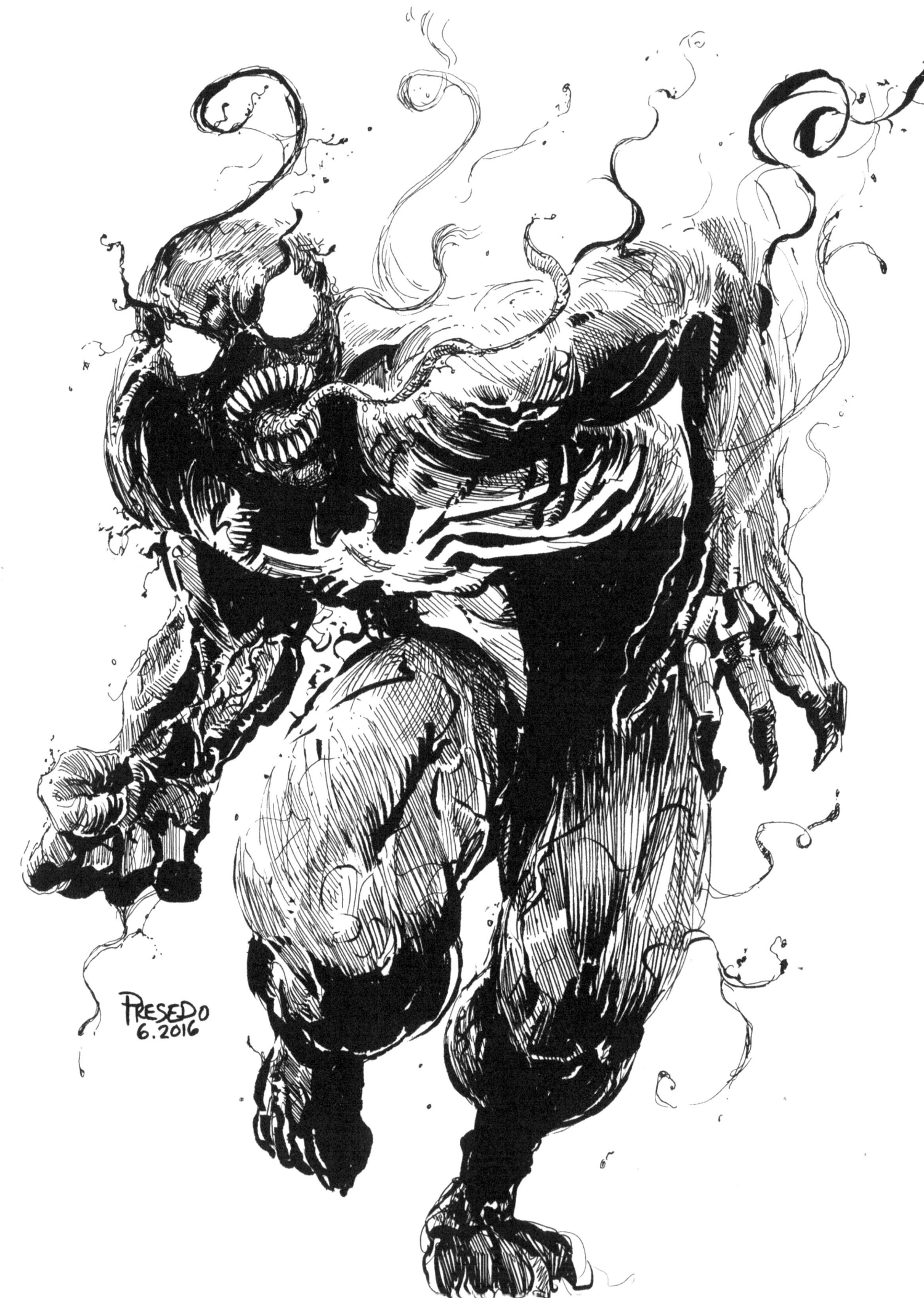

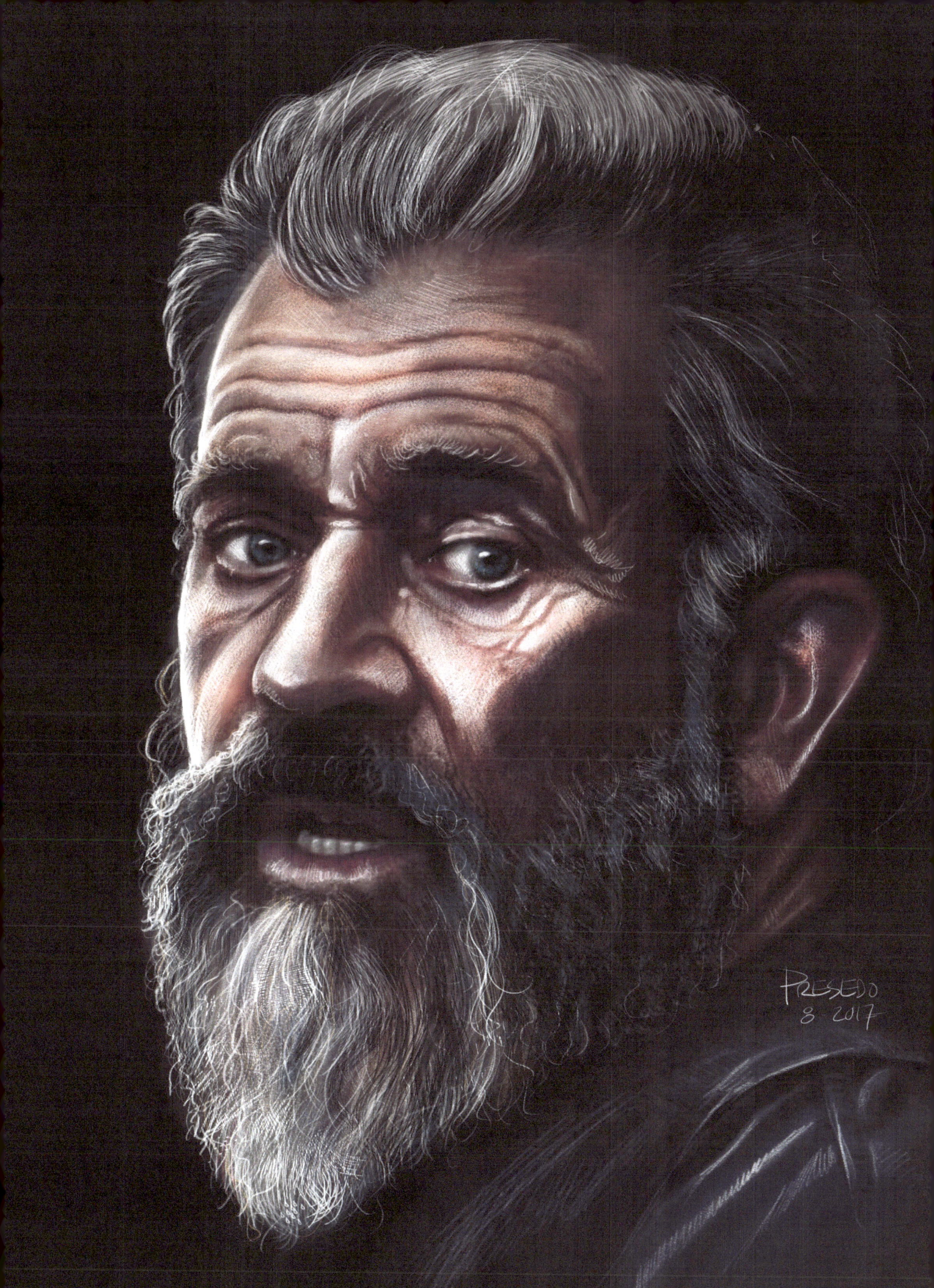

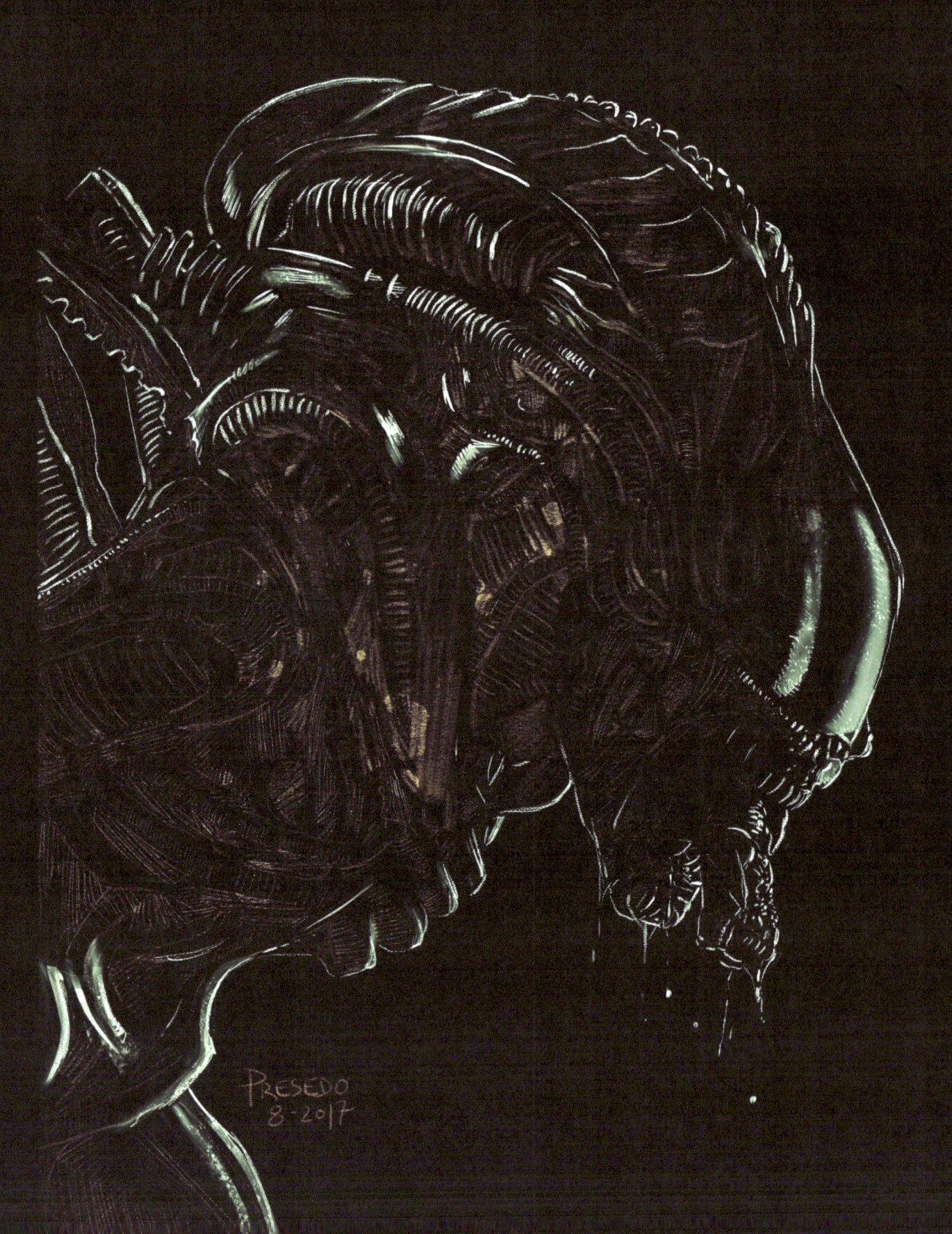

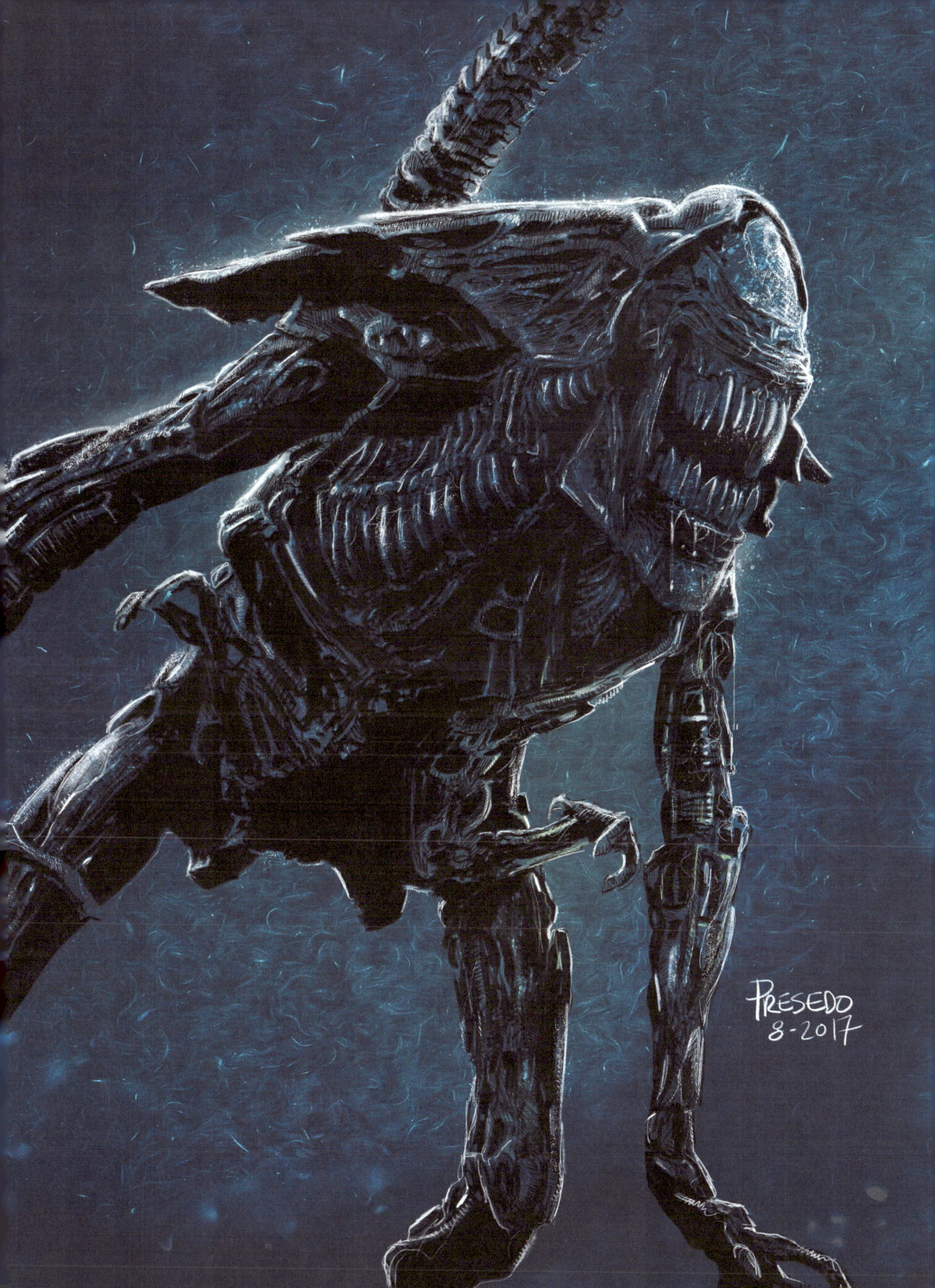

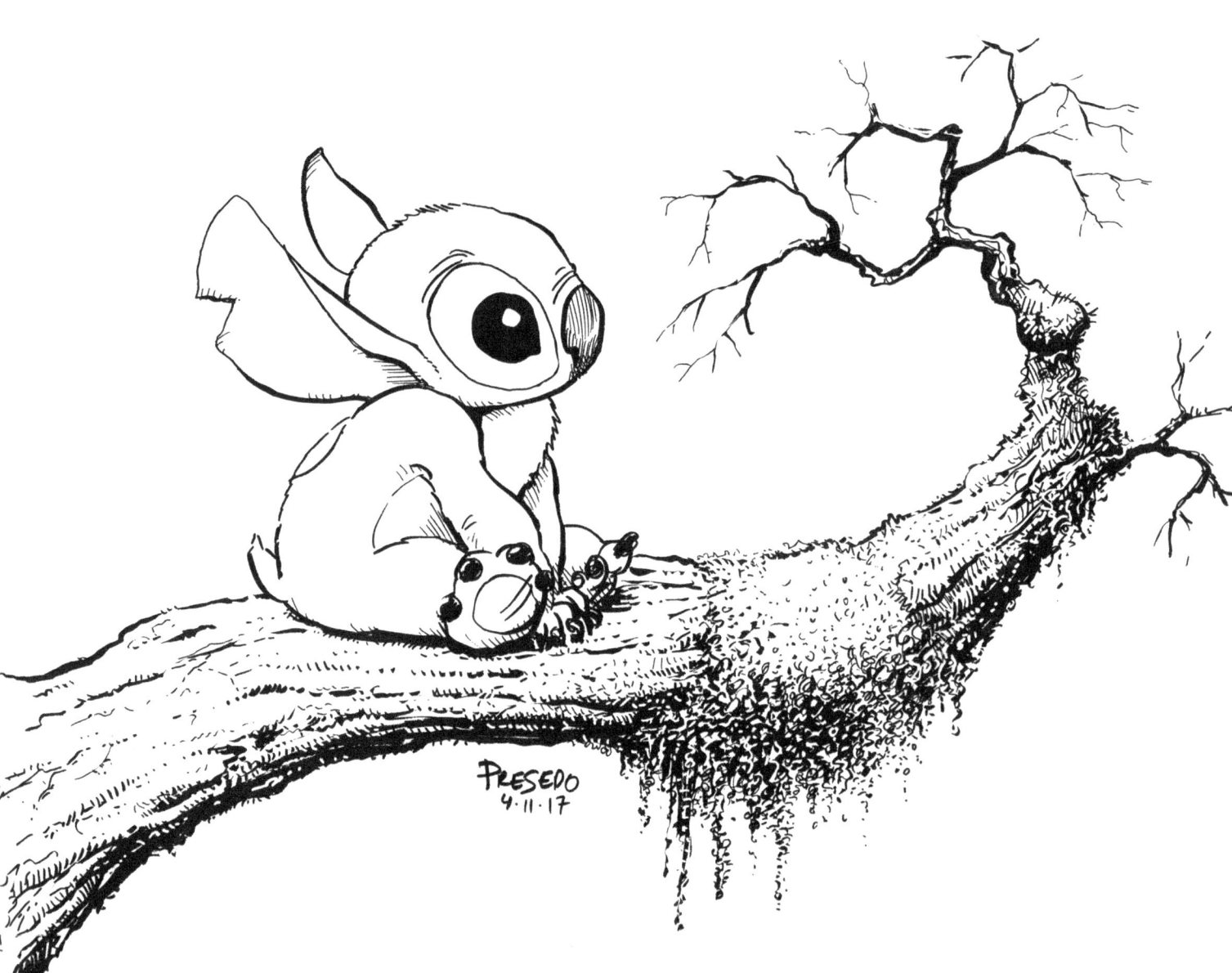

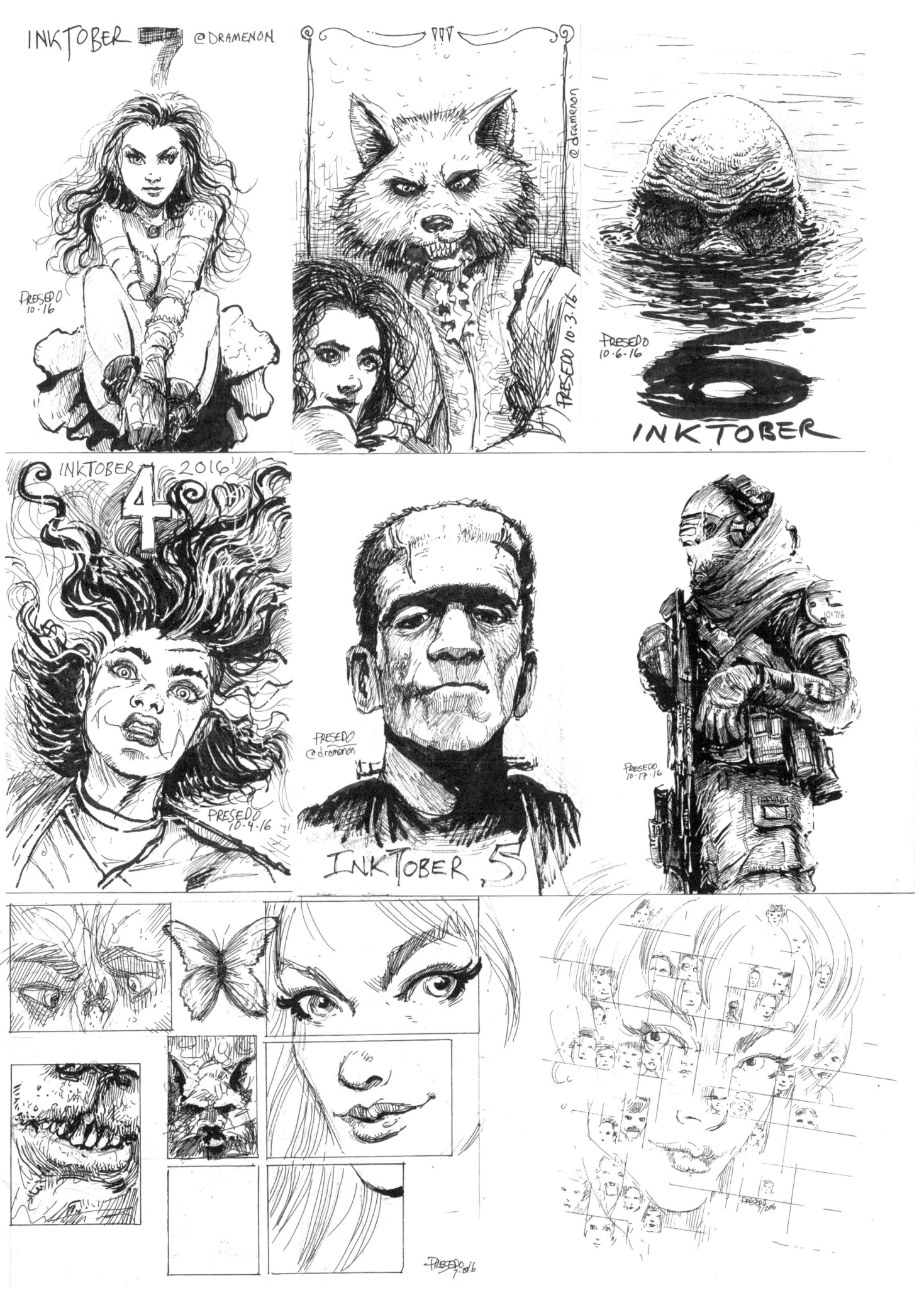

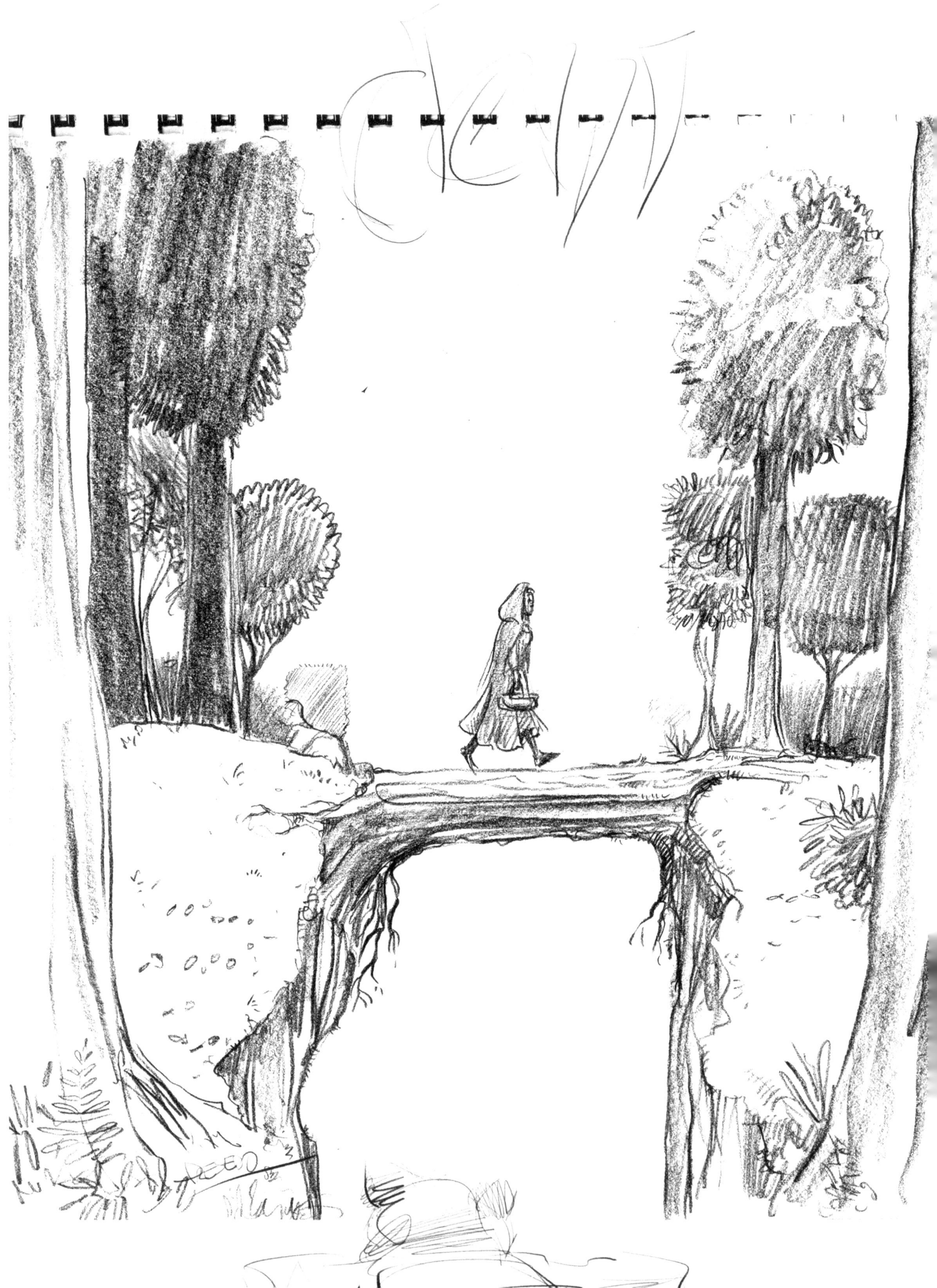

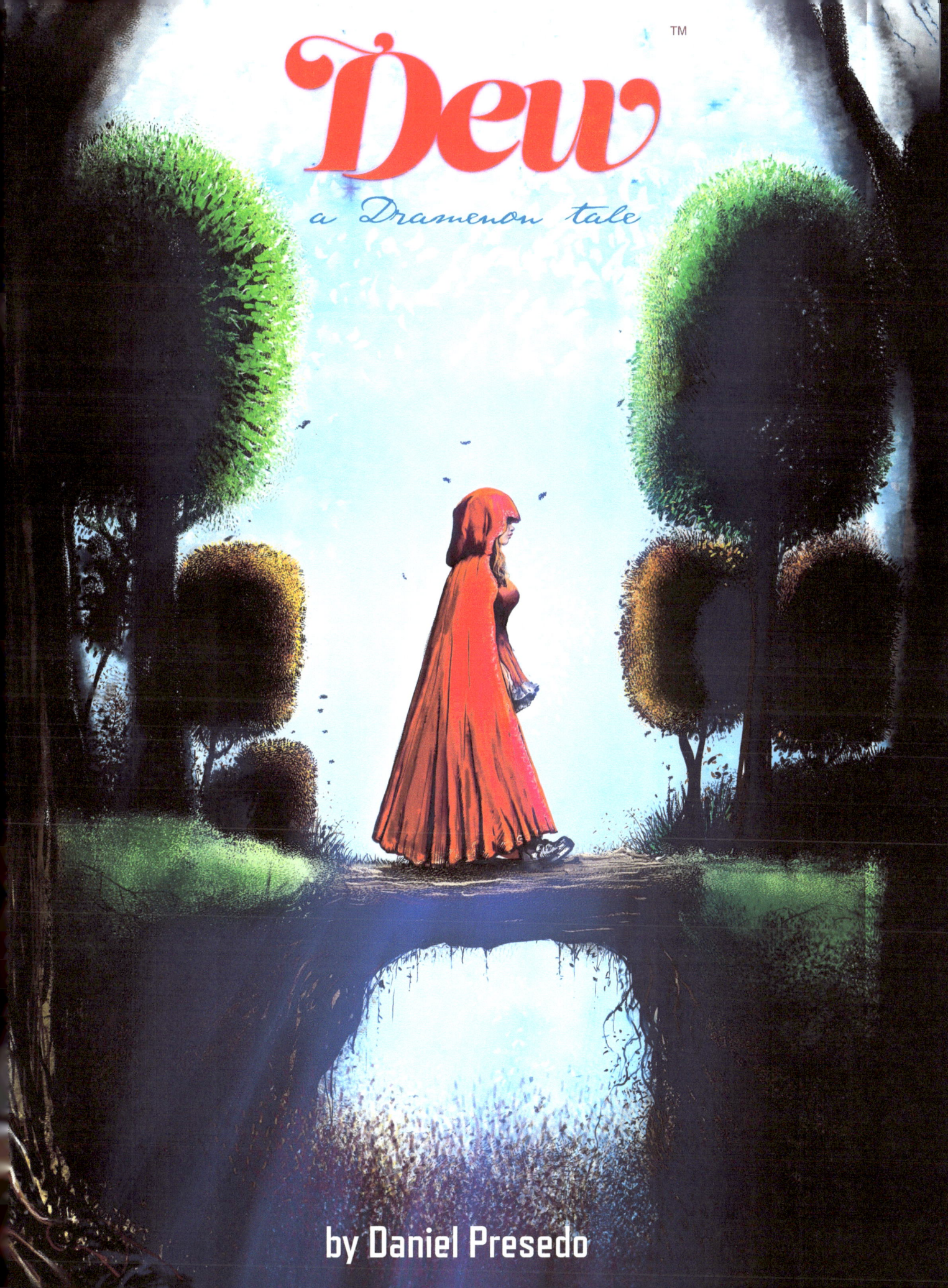

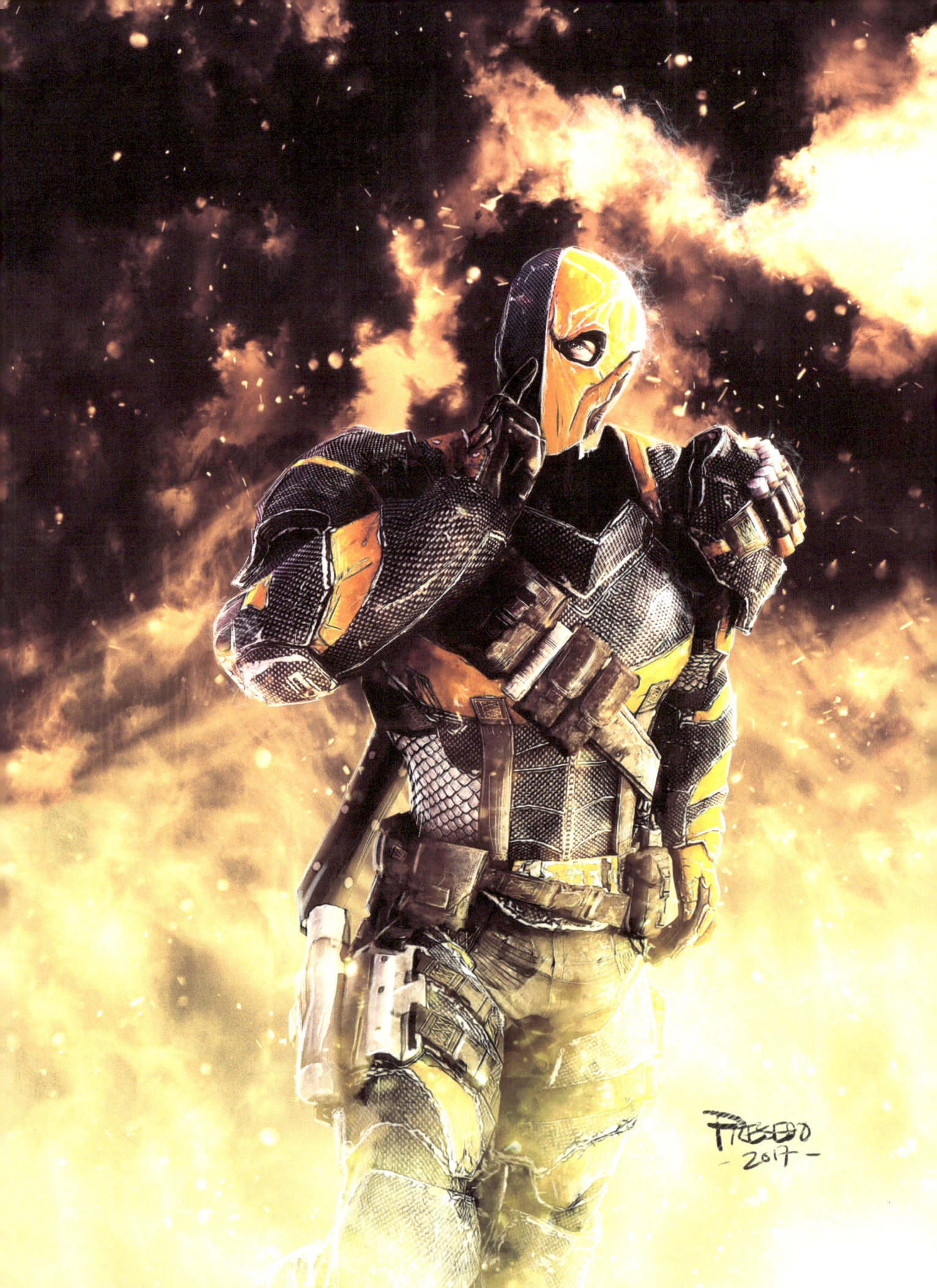

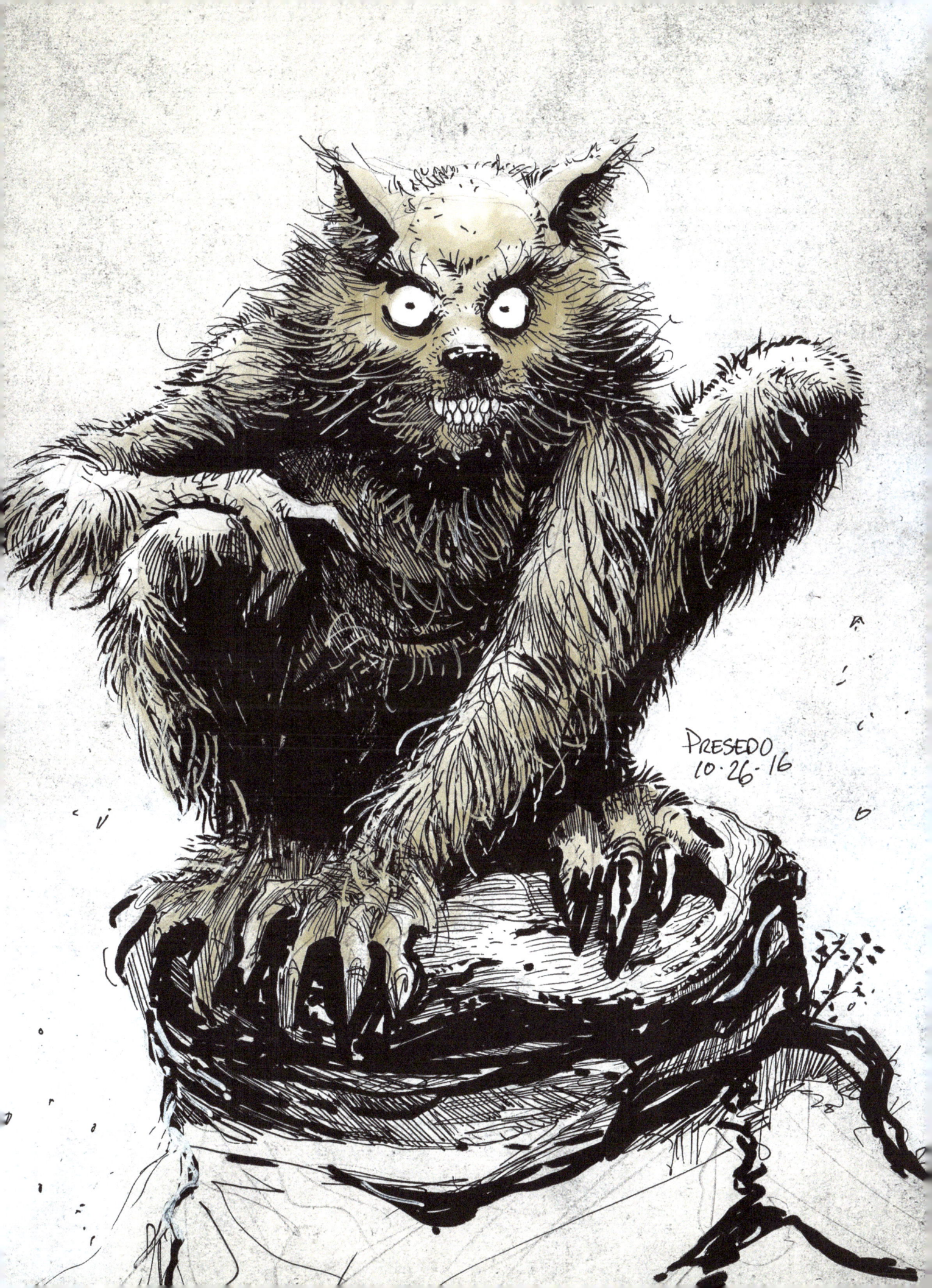

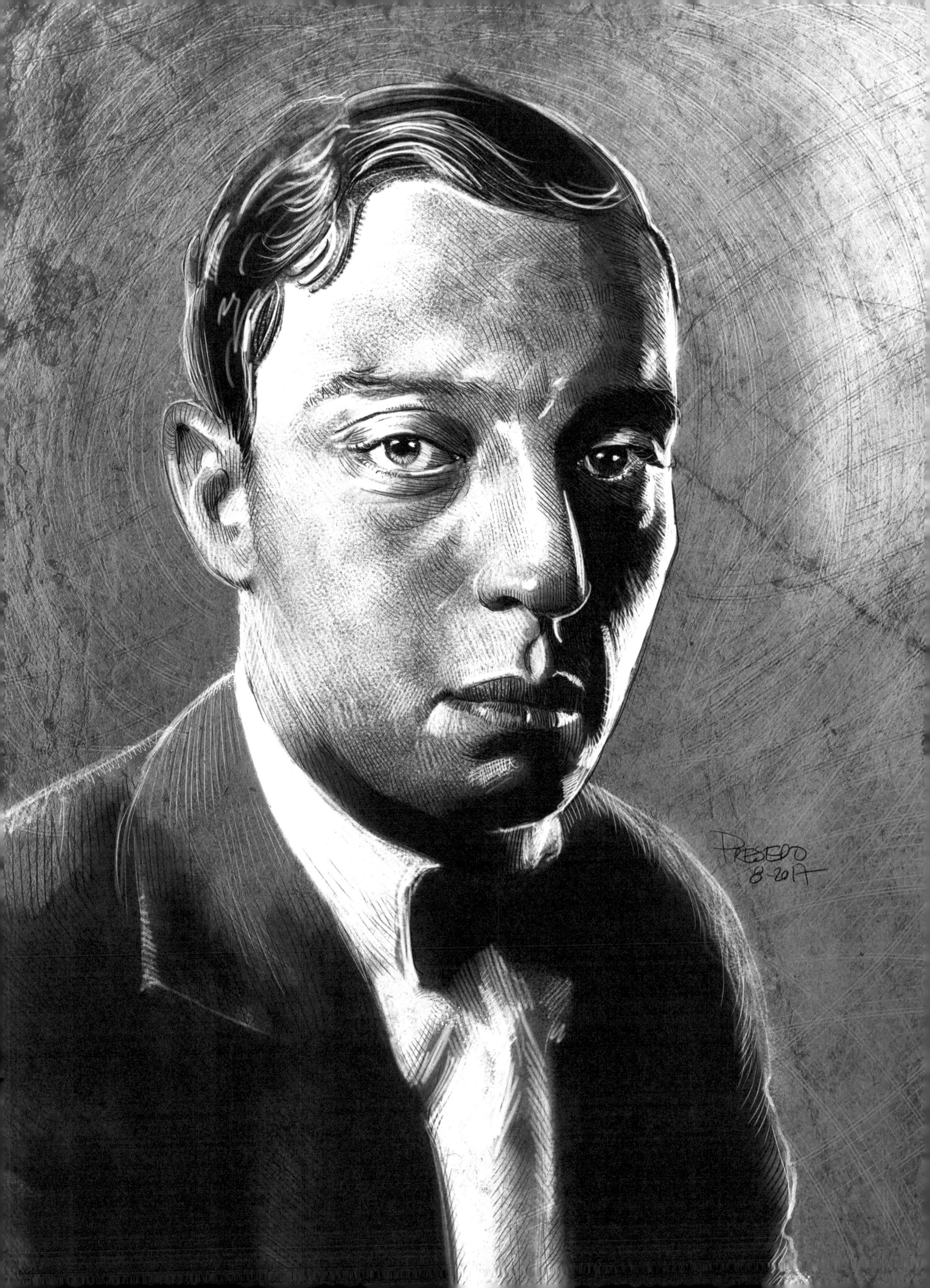

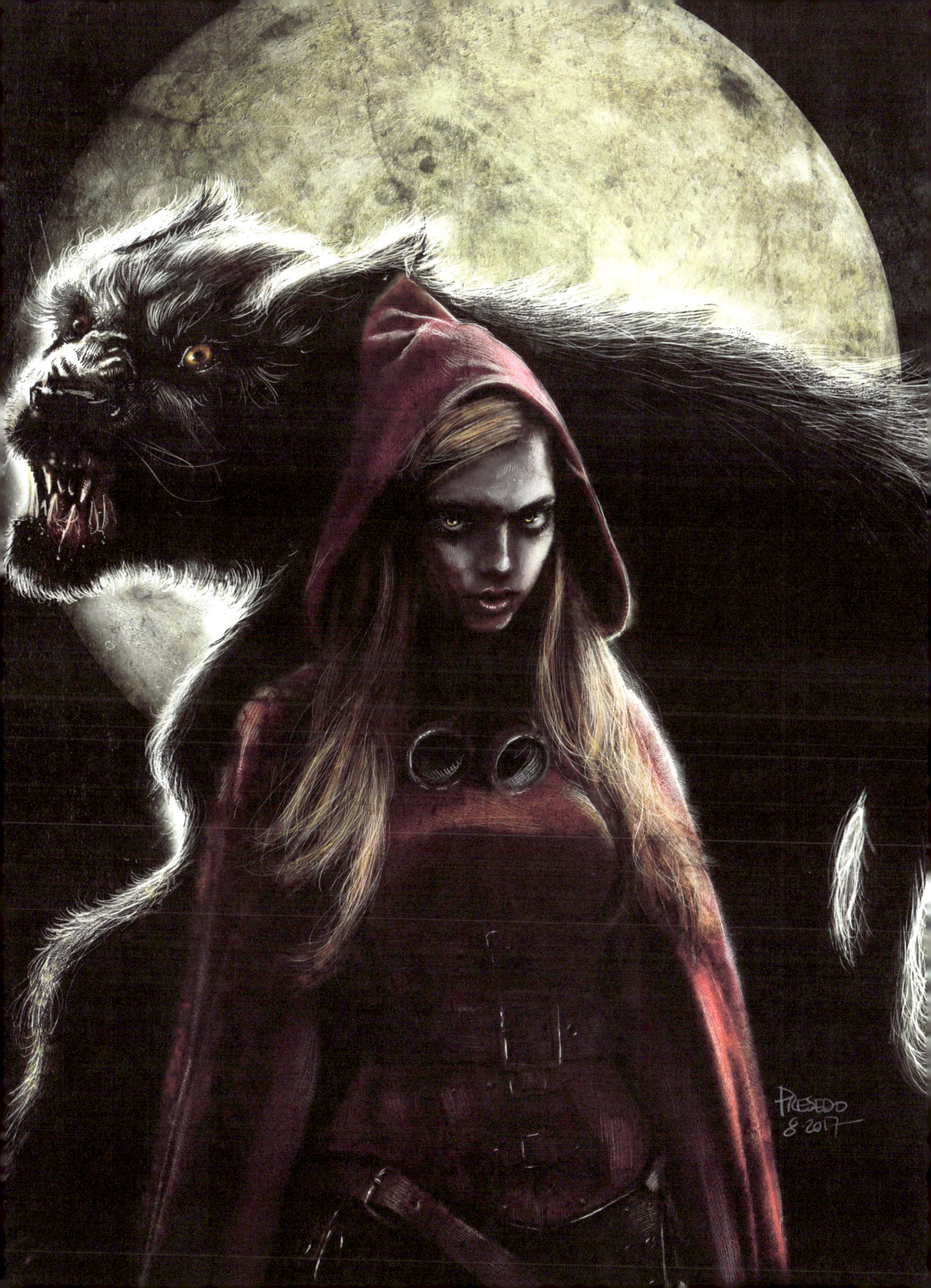

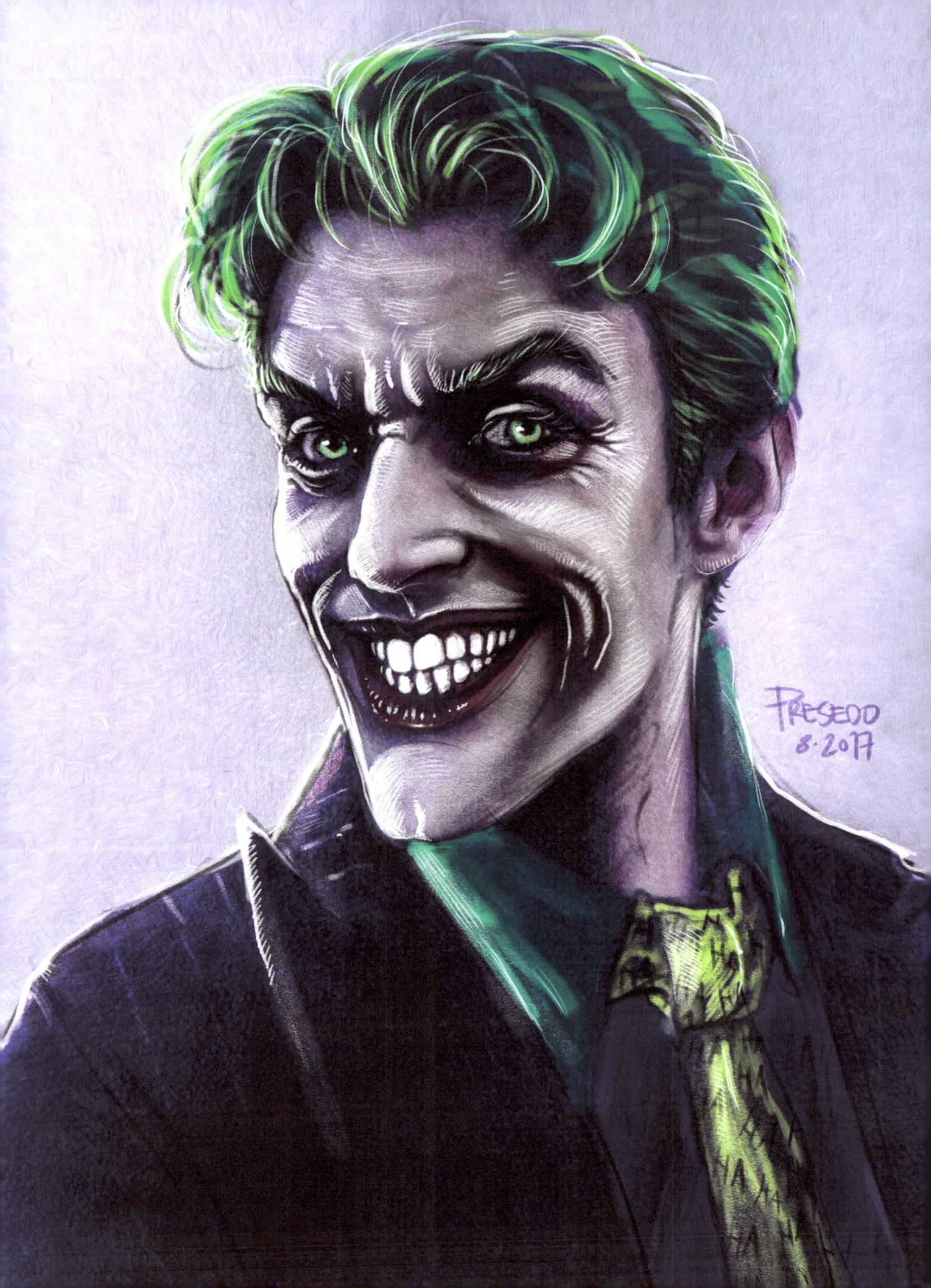

www.ingramcontent.com/pod-product-compliance
Lightning Source LLC
Chambersburg PA
CBHW051820210526
45473CB00005B/1680